Congressional Research Service

China-U.S. Trade Issues

Wayne M. Morrison
Specialist in Asian Trade and Finance

May 21, 2012

Congressional Research Service

7-5700

www.crs.gov

RL33536

CRS Report for Congress ————————————
Prepared for Members and Committees of Congress

Summary

U.S.-China economic ties have expanded substantially over the past three decades. Total U.S.-China trade rose from $5 billion in 1981 to $503 billion in 2011. China is currently the United States' second-largest trading partner, its third-largest export market, and its biggest source of imports. Because U.S. imports from China have risen much more rapidly than U.S. exports to China, the U.S. merchandise trade deficit has grown from $10 billion in 1990 to $296 billion in 2011. The rapid pace of economic integration between China and the United States, while benefiting both sides overall, has made the trade relationship increasingly complex. China's large population and booming economy have made it a large and growing market for U.S. exporters and investors. According to one estimate, China is currently a $200 billion market for U.S. firms. U.S. imports of low-cost goods from China greatly benefit U.S. consumers, and U.S. firms that use China as the final point of assembly for their products, or use Chinese-made inputs for production in the United States, are able to lower costs and become more globally competitive. China's purchases of U.S. Treasury securities (which total nearly $1.2 trillion) help keep U.S. interest rates relatively low. On the other hand, many analysts argue that growing commercial ties with China have exposed many U.S. firms to greater competition from low-cost Chinese firms, which they contend has negatively affected wages and employment in a number of U.S. industries.

However, China's incomplete transition to a free market economy and its use of distortive economic policies have increasingly strained commercial relations with the United States. Major concerns raised by U.S. policymakers and stakeholders include China's efforts to maintain an undervalued currency, its mixed record on implementing its World Trade Organization (WTO) obligations, its relatively poor record on protecting intellectual property rights (IPR), and its extensive use of industrial policies (such as financial support of state-owned firms, discriminatory government regulations, pressure on foreign-invested firms in China to transfer technology, and export restrictions on raw materials). Many analysts argue that such policies are harmful to U.S. economic interests and have contributed to U.S job losses. For example, one U.S. government study estimated that IPR infringement in China cost U.S. IPR-intensive firms $48 billion in 2009.

Some Members of Congress advocate a more aggressive U.S. trade policy towards China, such as increasing the number of dispute settlement cases brought against China in the WTO, where the United States has prevailed on a number of issues. During his State of the Union Address in January 2012, President Obama announced plans to create a new Trade Enforcement Unit "charged with investigating unfair trade practices in countries like China." Some analysts caution that taking a more aggressive stance against China over its trade policies could induce it to retaliate against U.S. exports to, and investment in, China. They further contend that major economic disputes should be dealt with through established high-level bilateral dialogues, such as the Strategic & Economic Dialogue (S&ED) and the U.S.-China Joint Commission on Commerce and Trade (JCCT). They note, for example, that under talks held under these forums, China agreed to eliminate discriminatory government procurement practices linked to the development of "indigenous innovation." Many trade observers contend that the United States should also continue to press China to rebalance its economic growth model by boosting domestic consumption and decreasing the country's reliance on exporting for its economic growth.

This report provides an overview of U.S.-China trade ties and major issues.

Contents

Figures

Tables

Contacts

E conomic and trade reforms begun in 1979 have helped transform China into one of the world's fastest-growing economies. China's economic growth and trade liberalization, including comprehensive trade commitments made upon entering the World Trade Organization (WTO) in 2001, have led to a sharp expansion in U.S.-China commercial ties. Yet, bilateral trade relations have become increasingly strained in recent years over a number of issues, including a large and growing U.S. trade deficit with China, resistance by China to reforming its currency policy, U.S. concerns over China's mixed record on implementing its WTO obligations, and numerous Chinese industrial policies that appear to impose new restrictions on foreign firms. Several Members of Congress have called on the Obama Administration to take a tougher stance against China to induce it to eliminate economic policies deemed harmful to U.S. economic interests and/or inconsistent with WTO rules. This report provides an overview of U.S.-China trade relations, surveys major trade disputes, and lists bills introduced in Congress that could affect bilateral commercial ties.

Most Recent Developments

On May 4, 2012, the United States and China concluded the fourth round of discussions held under the Strategic and Economic Dialogue (S&ED). China pledged to continue its efforts to rebalance its economy and to increase foreign access to certain financial services.

On April 14, 2012, China announced that it had widened the daily trading limit of its currency, the renminbi (RMB) against the dollar from 0.5% to 1%, a move many analysts contend could enhance the RMB's flexibility.

On March 13, 2012, the United States, Japan, and the European Union jointly initiated a WTO dispute resolution case against China over its export restrictions on rare earths (as well as tungsten and molybdenum).

During the visit to the United States by Chinese Vice President Xi Jinping (February 13-17, 2012), China agreed that it would expand market access for American movies, open up its mandatory third-party liability insurance sector for autos to foreign firms, and hold bilateral talks on establishing international guidelines for export financing.

On January 30, 2012, a WTO Appellate Body ruled that China's export quotas and duties on certain raw materials were inconsistent with its WTO obligations. The case was originally brought by the United States in 2009.

During his State of the Union Address on January 24, 2012, President Obama announced that he would create a new federal Trade Enforcement Unit "charged with investigating unfair trade practices in countries like China." On February 28, 2012, President Obama issued an executive order establishing an Interagency Trade Enforcement Center within the USTR's office.

U.S. Trade with China[1]

U.S.-China trade rose rapidly after the two nations reestablished diplomatic relations (in January 1979), signed a bilateral trade agreement (July 1979), and provided mutual most-favored-nation (MFN) treatment beginning in 1980.[2] In 1979 (when China's economic reforms began), total U.S.-China trade (exports plus imports) was $2 billion; China ranked as the United States' 23rd-largest export market and its 45th-largest source of imports. In 2011, bilateral merchandise trade was $503 billion; China was the second-largest U.S. trading partner (after Canada), the third-largest U.S. export market (after Canada and Mexico), and the largest source of U.S. imports. In recent years, China has been one of the fastest-growing U.S. export markets, and the importance of this market is expected to grow even further, given the pace of China's economic growth, and as Chinese living standards continue to improve and a sizable Chinese middle class emerges.

The U.S. trade deficit with China has surged over the past two decades, as U.S. imports from China have grown much faster than U.S. exports to China. That deficit rose from $10 billion in 1990 to $266 billion in 2008, fell to $227 billion in 2009,[3] then rose to $273 billion in 2010 and to $296 billion in 2011 (see **Table 1** and **Figure 1**).[4] As can be seen in **Figure 2**, the U.S. trade deficit with China in 2011 was significantly larger than that with any other U.S. trading partner and several trading groups. For example, it was larger than the combined U.S. trade deficits with the Organization of the Petroleum Exporting Countries (OPEC), the 27 nations that make up the European Union (EU27), and the 10 nations that make up the Association of Southeast Asian Nations (ASEAN). Some Members contend that the large U.S. trade deficit is an indicator that the trade relationship is unbalanced, unfair, and damaging to the U.S. economy. In the 112th Congress, H.R. 2909 (Sherman) would terminate China's normal trade relations status and would direct the President to negotiate a new trade agreement with China in order to achieve a balance of trade in four years.

---

[1] For more information on China's economy, see CRS Report RL33534, *China's Economic Conditions*, by Wayne M. Morrison. For general information on U.S.-China political ties, see CRS Report R41108, *U.S.-China Relations: Policy Issues*, by Susan V. Lawrence and Thomas Lum.

[2] The United States suspended China's MFN status in 1951, which cut off most bilateral trade. China's MFN status was conditionally restored in 1980 under the provisions set forth under Title IV of the 1974 Trade Act, as amended (including the Jackson-Vanik freedom-of-emigration provisions). China's MFN status (which was re-designated under U.S. trade law as normal trade relations status, or NTR) was renewed on an annual basis until January 2002, when permanent NTR was extended to China (after it joined the WTO in December 2001).

[3] The decline in the U.S. trade deficit with China was largely due to the effects of the global economic downturn that began in 2008.

[4] The U.S. trade deficit for January-March 2012 was up 11.5% over the same period in 2011. If this trend continues, the total U.S. trade deficit with China in 2012 could rise to around $340 billion.

Table 1. U.S. Merchandise Trade with China:
1980-2011

(\$ billions)

Year	U.S. Exports	U.S. Imports	U.S. Trade Balance
1980	3.8	1.1	2.7
1985	3.9	3.9	0.0
1990	4.8	15.2	-10.4
1995	11.7	45.6	-33.8
2000	16.3	100.1	-83.8
2005	41.8	243.5	-201.6
2006	55.2	287.8	-232.5
2007	65.2	321.5	-256.3
2008	71.5	337.8	-266.3
2009	69.6	296.4	-226.8
2010	91.9	364.9	-273.1
2011	103.9	393.3	-295.5

Source: U.S. International Trade Commission (USITC) DataWeb.

Figure 1. U.S. Merchandise Trade With China: 2002-2011

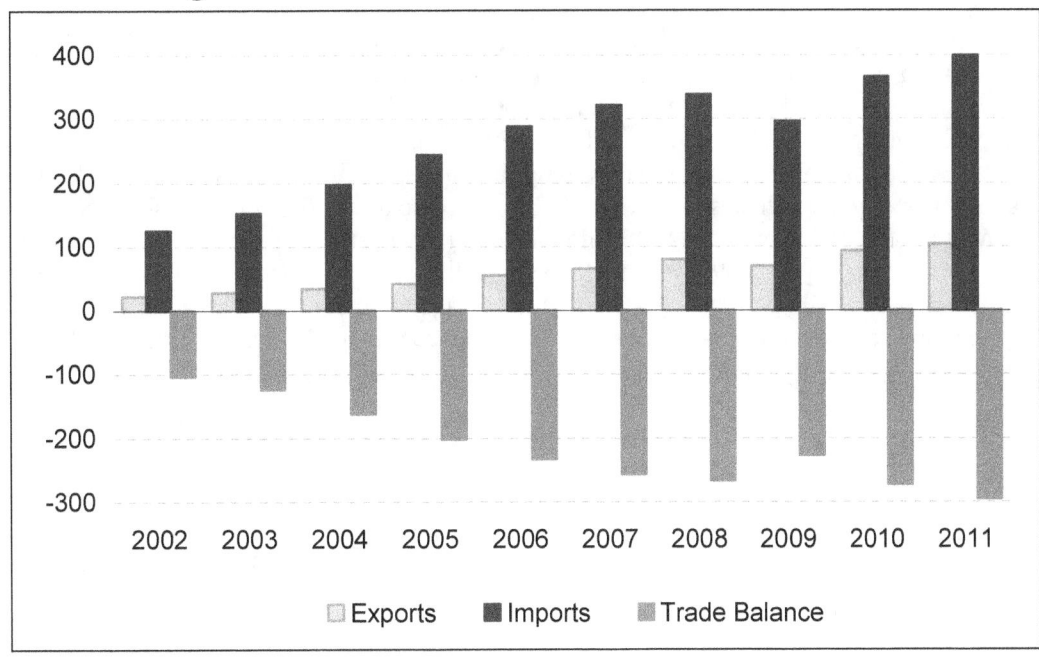

Source: U. S. International Trade Commission DataWeb.

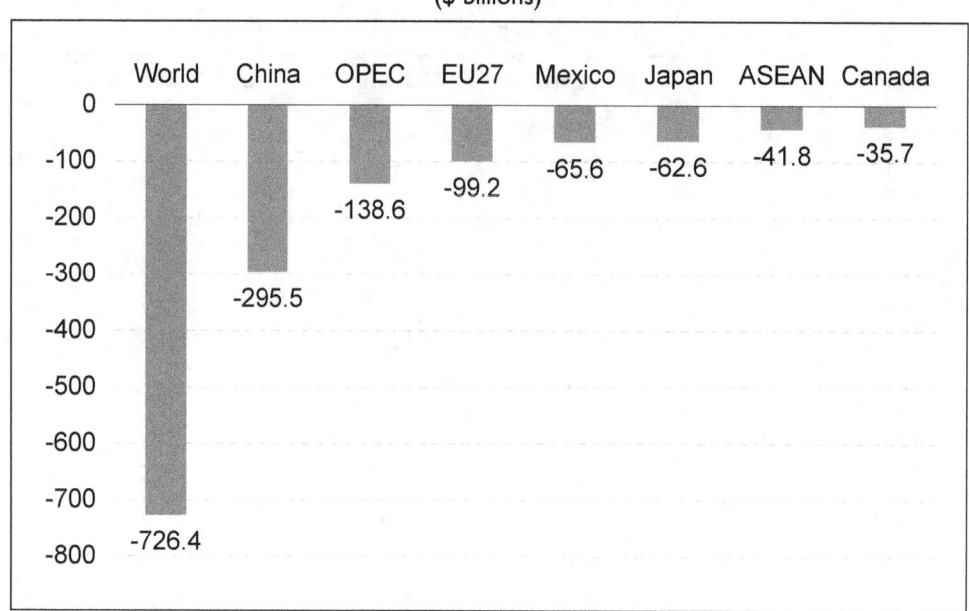

Figure 2. U.S. Trade Balances with Trading Partners: 2011

($ billions)

Source: U.S. International Trade Commission DataWeb.

U.S. Merchandise Exports to China

U.S. merchandise exports to China in 2011 were $103.9 billion, up 13.1% over 2010 levels.[5] China replaced Japan as the third-largest U.S. merchandise export market in 2007 and has remained so through 2011 (see **Figure 3**). From 2000 to 2011, the share of total U.S. exports going to China rose from 2.1% to 7.0%.[6] The top five merchandise U.S. exports to China in 2011 were waste and scrap, oilseeds and grains, aircraft and parts, semiconductors and other electronic components, and motor vehicles (see **Table 2**). China is also a significant market for U.S. exports of private services, which totaled $21.1 billion in 2010 (the most recent year available), which was a 35.3% increase over 2009 levels, making China the seventh-largest export market for U.S. private services. According to the U.S.-China Business Council, the total market for the sale of U.S. goods and services in China (i.e., U.S. exports and sales by U.S.-invested firms in China) could be as high as $200 billion annually.[7]

---

[5] This was a slowdown from 2010 when U.S. exports to China increased by 32.1% over the previous year.

[6] However, China's share of U.S. exports in 2011 was lower than the 7.2% level that occurred in 201.

[7] The U.S. China Business, *The President's 2012 Trade Agenda, Testimony by John Frisibie, President, U.S.-China Business Council to the Senate Finance Committee*, March 7, 2012.

Figure 3. Top 5 U.S. Export Markets: 2011

($ billions)

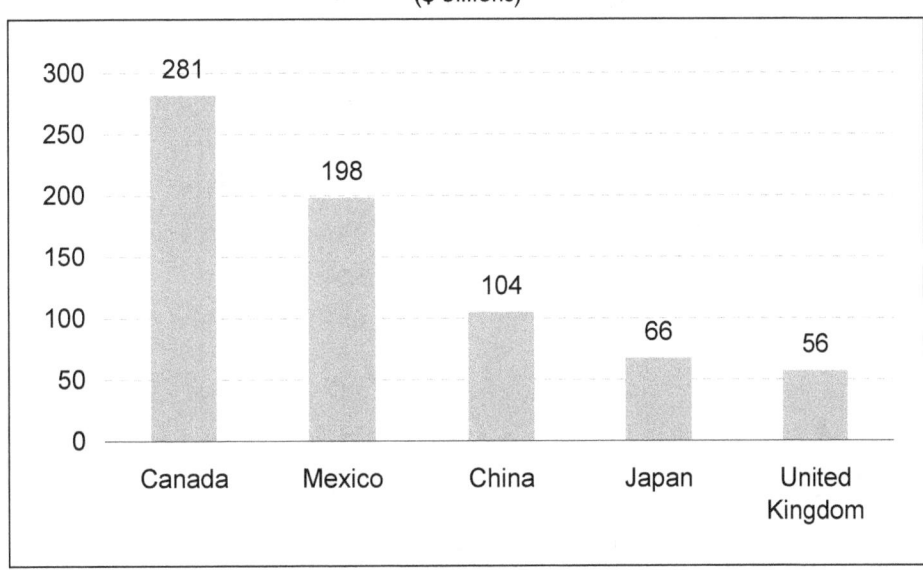

Source: U.S. International Trade Commission DataWeb.

Although U.S. exports to China slowed somewhat in 2011 relative to previous years (and compared with the growth in U.S. exports to other major trading partners), when measured over a 10-year period, China has been by far one of the fastest-growing U.S. export markets, as seen in **Table 3**. From 2002 to 2011, U.S. exports to China increased by about 471% (the overall growth in U.S. exports over this period was 213.6%).[8]

---

[8] During the first three months of 2012, U.S. merchandise exports to China were up by 3.6% over the same period in 2011, which was slower than the rise of total U.S. exports (at 8.7%).

Table 2. Major U.S. Exports to China: 2007-2011

($ millions and percent change)

NAIC Commodity	2007	2008	2009	2010	2011	2010-2011 Percent Change
Total Exports to China	**65,238**	**71,457**	**69,576**	**91,878**	**103,879**	**13.1%**
Waste and scrap	7,331	7,562	7,142	8,561	11,540	34.8%
Oilseeds and grains	4,145	7,316	9,376	11,208	11,500	2.6%
Aerospace products and parts	7,447	5,471	5,344	5,766	6,392	10.9%
Semiconductors and other electronic components	7,435	7,475	6,041	7,555	5,668	-25.0%
Motor vehicles	908	1,194	1,134	3,515	5,369	52.7%
Basic chemicals	2,914	3,090	3,433	4,202	4,658	10.8%
Resin, synthetic rubber, & artificial & synthetic fibers & filament	3,290	3,524	4,036	4,336	4,476	3.2%
Navigational, measuring ,electro-medical, and control instruments	2,444	2,886	2,917	3,782	4,275	13.0%
Other general purpose machinery	1,885	2,273	1,890	2,445	3,113	27.3%
Other agricultural products	1,558	1,786	1,008	2,328	2,825	21.4%

Source: USITC DataWeb.

Note: Top 10 U.S. exports to China in 2011using the North American Industry Classification (NAIC) System on a 4-digit level.

Table 3. Major U.S. Merchandise Export Markets in 2011

($ billions and percent change)

	2002	2010	2011	2010-2011 Percent Change	2002-2011 Percent Change
Total Global U.S. Exports	693.3	1,277.5	1,480.6	15.9%	213.6%
Canada	160.8	248.2	280.8	13.1%	174.6%
Mexico	97.5	163.3	197.5	21.0%	202.5%
China	22.1	91.9	103.9	13.1%	471.0%
Japan	51.4	60.5	66.2	9.3%	128.6%
United Kingdom	33.3	48.5	56.0	15.4%	168.3%
Germany	26.6	48.2	49.1	1.9%	184.5%
Korea	22.6	38.8	43.5	12.0%	192.5%
Brazil	12.4	35.4	42.9	21.5%	346.1%
Netherlands	18.3	35.0	42.8	22.4%	233.6%
Hong Kong	12.6	26.6	36.5	37.4%	289.5%

Source: U.S. International Trade Commission DataWeb.

Many trade analysts argue that China could prove to be a much more significant market for U.S. exports in the future. China is one of the world's fastest-growing economies, and rapid economic growth is likely to continue in the near future, provided that economic reforms are continued.[9] China's goals of modernizing its infrastructure, upgrading its industries, and improving rural living standards could generate substantial demand for foreign goods and services. Finally, economic growth has substantially improved the purchasing power of Chinese citizens, especially those living in urban areas along the east coast of China. China's growing economy, large foreign exchange reserves (at over $3.2 trillion as of December 2011), and large population of over 1.3 billion people make it a potentially enormous market. To illustrate:

- According to a report by the Boston Consulting Group, in 2009, China had 148 million "middle class and affluent" consumers, defined as those whose annual household income was 60,000 RMB ($9,160) or higher, and that level is projected to rise to 415 million by 2020.[10] According to Bloomberg News, China had an estimated 1.1 million millionaires (converted to U.S. dollars) in 2010.[11]

- Although Chinese private consumption as a percent of GDP is much lower than that of most other major economies, the rate of growth of Chinese private consumption has been rising rapidly. For example, private consumption as a percent of GDP in China in 2011 was 34.0%, compared to 71.1% in the United States. However, the annual rate of growth in Chinese private consumption from 2002 to 2011 averaged 8.0%, while the U.S. annual average was 1.9%.

- China's government has indicated that it plans to step up efforts to boost domestic spending to help lessen its dependence on exports as the major contributor to China's economic growth. In 2008, China began the implementation of a $586 billion economic stimulus package, largely focused on infrastructure projects. China's goals of developing its western regions, expanding and modernizing its infrastructure, boosting its social safety net (such as health care and pensions), modernizing and developing key industries, reducing pollution, and raising incomes of the rural poor will likely result in large-scale government spending levels.[12] China's 12th Five-Year Plan (2011-2015) reportedly will allocate $1 trillion in infrastructure spending.

- China currently has the world's largest mobile phone network and one of the fastest-growing markets, with over 1 billion mobile phone subscribers as of March 2012, up from 87 million subscribers in 2000.[13]

---

[9] China's real GDP growth from 2008 to 2011 averaged 9.6%.

[10] Boston Consulting Group, *Big Prizes in Small Places: China's Rapidly Multiplying Pockets of Growth,* November 2010, p. 10.

[11] *Bloomberg*, "China's Millionaires Jump Past 1 Million on Savings, Expansion of Economy," June 1, 2011.

[12] The Chinese government's ability to fund these projects is enhanced by the fact that its debt levels are much smaller relatively to those of other major economies. For example, China's central government budget deficit as a percent of GDP in 2011 was 1.6% versus 8.7% for the United States. China's public debt as a percent of GDP at the end of 2011 was 16.1% versus 66.1% for the United States. Source: *Economist Intelligence Unit*, Country Data, database.

[13] China Daily, "China Mobile phone users exceed 1 billion," March 20, 2012, at http://www.chinadaily.com.cn/china/2012-03/30/content_14954435.htm.

- Boeing Corporation predicts that over the next 20 years (2011-2030), China will buy 5,000 new commercial airplanes valued at $600 billion and will be Boeing's largest commercial airplane customer outside the United States.[14]

- China replaced the United States as the world's largest Internet user in 2008. At the end of December 2011, China had an estimated 513 million users versus 245 million in the United States.[15] Yet, the percentage of the Chinese population using the Internet is small relative to the United States: 38.4% versus 78.3%, respectively.

- According to *Global Insight*, China reportedly overtook Japan in 2009 to become the largest producer of light vehicles (cars and light trucks) at 12.9 million units and overtook the United States as the global leader in sales of light vehicles at 13.0 million units.[16] China's light vehicle sales nearly doubled from 2008 to 2010 (due largely to government tax subsidies and incentives that were implemented in response to the global economic slowdown). By 2021, sales of light vehicles in China are projected to reach 31.5 million units, which would be nearly double the projected sales in the United States. The number of cars on the road in China rose from 14 million units in 2005 to an estimated 55.9 million units 2011, and is projected to reach 131.6 million by 2016, a level that would equal 96.1% of the projected number of cars on the road in the United States.[17]

- For the first time in its history, General Motors (GM) in 2010 sold more cars and trucks in China (at 2.35 million units) than it did in the United States (2.21 million units).[18] In 2011, GM sold 2.55 million vehicles in China (up 8.3% over 2010 levels) versus 2.50 million in the United States. GM in China currently has 11 joint ventures and two wholly owned foreign enterprises and employs more than 35,000 workers.[19]

Major U.S. Imports from China

China was the largest source of U.S. merchandise imports in 2011, at $399.3 billion. U.S. imports from China increased by 9.4% in 2011 (compared to 23.1% rise in 2010) over the previous year. China's share of total U.S. imports rose from 8.2% in 2000 to 19.1% in 2010, but dropped to 18.1% in 2011. The importance (ranking) of China as a source of U.S. imports has risen sharply, from eighth largest in 1990, to fourth in 2000, to second in 2004-2006, to first in 2007-2012. The top five U.S. imports from China in 2011 were computer equipment, communications equipment, miscellaneous manufactured products (such as toys and games), apparel, and semiconductors and other electronic parts (see **Table 4**).[20] From January to March 2012, U.S. imports from China were up 9.0% over the same period in 2011.

---

[14] Boeing Corporation, *Current Market Outlook: 2011-2030*, June 2011.

[15] Internet World Stats, at http://www.internetworldstats.com/stats htm.

[16] HIS Global Insight, *World Car Industry Forecast Report*, September 2011.

[17] For additional information on the U.S. auto industry in China, see CRS Report R40924, *The Rise of China's Auto Industry and Its Impact on the U.S. Motor Vehicle Industry*, by Rachel Tang.

[18] USA Today, *GM sells more vehicles in China than in U.S*, January 21, 2011.

[19] According to GM's website, it currently has 11 joint ventures and two wholly owned foreign enterprises in China where it employees more than 35,000 workers.

[20] China has become a growing source of U.S. private services imports; these totaled $10 billion in 2010, making China (continued...)

Table 4. Major U.S. Imports From China: 2007-2011

(\$ millions and percent change)

NAIC Commodity	2007	2008	2009	2010	2011	2010-2011 Percent Change
Computer equipment	44,462	45,820	44,818	59,800	68,276	14.2%
Communications equipment	23,192	26,618	26,362	33,464	39,806	19.0%
Miscellaneous manufactured commodities	34,827	35,835	30,668	34,168	32,672	-4.4%
Apparel	22,955	22,583	22,669	26,603	27,554	3.6%
Semiconductors and other electronic components	15,353	13,645	12,363	18,263	19,835	8.6%
Footwear	13,929	14,230	13,119	15,673	16,482	5.2%
Audio and video equipment	19,075	19,715	18,253	19,493	15,853	-18.7%
Household and institutional furniture and kitchen cabinets	11,872	11,086	9,128	11,123	11,398	2.5%
Household appliances and miscellaneous machines	8,266	8,520	7,724	9,090	9,569	5.3%
Other fabricated metal products	6,781	7,242	5,690	7,228	8,638	19.5%
Total imports from China	321,508	337,790	296,402	364,944	399,335	9.4%

Source: U.S. International Trade Commission DataWeb.

Notes: Top 10 U.S. imports from China in 2011 using the North American Industry Classification (NAIC) System on a 4-digit level.

Throughout the 1980s and 1990s, nearly all U.S. imports from China were low-value, labor-intensive products, such as toys and games, consumer electronic products, footwear, and textiles and apparel. However, over the past few years, an increasing proportion of U.S. imports from China have been comprised of more technologically advanced products (see text box below).

U.S.-China Trade in Advance Technology Products

According to the U.S. Census Bureau, U.S. imports of "advanced technology products" (ATP) from China in 2011 totaled \$129.5 billion. ATP products accounted for 32.4% of total U.S. imports from China, compared with 19.2% (\$29.3 billion) in 2003. In addition, ATP imports from China accounted for 33.5% of total U.S ATP imports (compared with 14.1% in 2003). U.S. ATP exports to China in 2011 were \$21.4 billion; these accounted for 20.6% of total U.S. exports to China and 7.5% of U.S. global ATP exports. In comparison, U.S. ATP exports to China in 2003 were \$8.3 billion, which accounted for 29.2% of U.S. exports to China and 4.6% of total U.S. ATP exports.

The United States ran a \$108.1 billion deficit in its ATP trade with China in 2011, up from a \$21.0 billion deficit in 2003. Some see the large and growing U.S. trade deficit in ATP with China as a source of concern, contending that it signifies the growing international competitiveness of China in high technology. Others dispute this, noting that a large share of the ATP imports from China are in fact relatively low-end technology products and parts, such as notebook computers, or are products that are assembled in China using imported high technology parts that are largely developed and/or made elsewhere.

(...continued)

the seventh-largest source of private services imports.

China as a Major Center for Global Supply Chains

Many analysts contend that the sharp increase in U.S. imports from China (and hence the growing bilateral trade imbalance) is largely the result of movement in production facilities from other (primarily Asian) countries to China. That is, various products that used to be made in such places as Japan, Taiwan, Hong Kong, etc., and then exported to the United States, are now being made in China (in many cases, by foreign firms in China). To illustrate, in 1990, 47.1% of the value of U.S. manufactured imports came from Pacific Rim countries (including China).[21] In 2011, Pacific Rim countries accounted for 46.1% of total U.S. manufactured imports. Over the same period, the share of total U.S. manufactured imports that came from China increased from 3.6% to 25.3%. In other words, while China was becoming an increasingly important source for U.S. manufactured imports, the relative importance of the rest of the Pacific Rim (as a whole) as a source of U.S. imports was declining, in part because many multinational firms were shifting their export-oriented manufacturing facilities to China (see **Figure 4**).[22]

Figure 4. U.S. Manufactured Imports from Pacific Rim Countries as a Percent of Total U.S. Manufactured Imports: 1990, 2000, and 2011

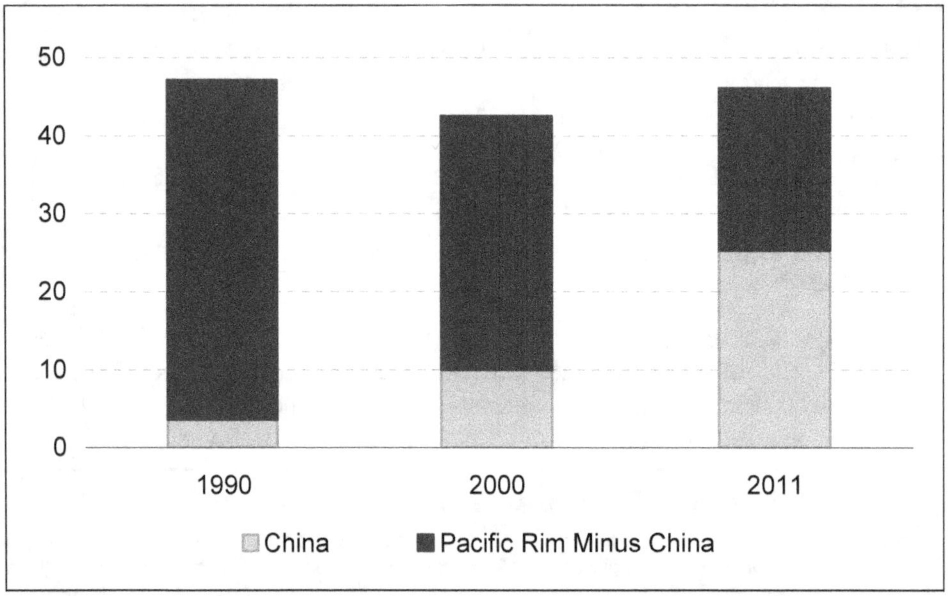

Source: U.S. International Trade Commission DataWeb.

Notes: Standard International Trade Classification (SITC) definition of manufactured imports.

Another illustration of the shift in production can be seen in the case of U.S. computer equipment imports, which constitute the largest category of U.S. imports from China (on an NAIC basis, 4-digit level). **Table 5** lists U.S. imports of computer equipment and parts from 2000-2011. In 2000, Japan was the largest foreign supplier of U.S. computer equipment (with a 19.6% share of total

---

[21] Pacific Rim countries include Australia, Brunei, Cambodia, China, Hong Kong, Indonesia, Japan, South Korea, Laos, Macao, Malaysia, New Zealand, North Korea, Papua New Guinea, the Philippines, Singapore, Taiwan, Thailand, Vietnam, and several small island nations.

[22] U.S. manufactured imports from Pacific Rim countries minus China as a percent of total U.S. manufactured imports fell from 43.5% in 1990 to 20.8% in 2011.

U.S. imports), while China ranked fourth (with a 12.1% share). By 2011, Japan's ranking had fallen to third; the value of its shipments dropped by 61.9% over 2000 levels, and its share of U.S. computer imports declined to 4.8% (2011). China was by far the largest foreign supplier of computer equipment in 2011 with a 64.4% share of total U.S. computer equipment imports, compared to 12.0% in 2000 (see **Figure 5**). While U.S. imports of computer equipment from China from 2000-2011 rose by 722.9%, the total value of U.S. computer imports worldwide rose by 57.7%.[23] A study by the U.S. International Trade Commission (USITC) estimated that in 2002 over 99% of computer exports in China were from foreign-invested firms in China.[24] Taiwan, one of the world's leaders in sales of information technology, produces over 90% its information hardware equipment (such as computers) in China. Computer equipment, like many other globally traded products, often involves many stages of production, using parts and other inputs made by numerous multinational firms throughout the world, a significant share of which is assembled in China. The globalization of supply chains makes it increasingly difficult to interpret conventional U.S. trade statistics (see **text box**).

Table 5. Major Foreign Suppliers of U.S. Computer Equipment Imports: 2000-2011

($ billions and percent change)

	2000	2002	2004	2006	2008	2010	2011	2000-2011 % change
Total	68.5	62.3	73.9	83.8	85.4	97.2	106.0	57.7%
China	**8.3**	**12.0**	**29.5**	**40.0**	**45.8**	**59.8**	**68.3**	**722.9%**
Mexico	6.9	7.9	7.4	6.6	6.2	13.6	14.5	110.1%
Japan	13.4	8.1	6.3	6.3	6.6	5.2	5.1	-61.9%
Singapore	8.7	7.1	6.6	5.6	4.0	3.6	3.2	-63.2%
Thailand	2.4	2.1	2.3	3.2	3.7	3.5	3.0	25.0%

Source: U.S. International Trade Commission Trade DataWeb.

Note: Ranked according to top five foreign suppliers of computer equipment imports in 2011.

[23] China's accession to the WTO (with the reduction of trade and investment barriers) appears to have been a major factor behind the migration of computer production from other countries to China.

[24] USITC, *How Much of Chinese Exports Is Really Made In China? Assessing Foreign and Domestic Value-Added in Gross Exports*, report number 2008-03-B, March 2008, p. 21.

**Figure 5. U.S. Computer Imports from China as a Percent of
U.S. Total Computer Imports: 2000-2011**

(percent)

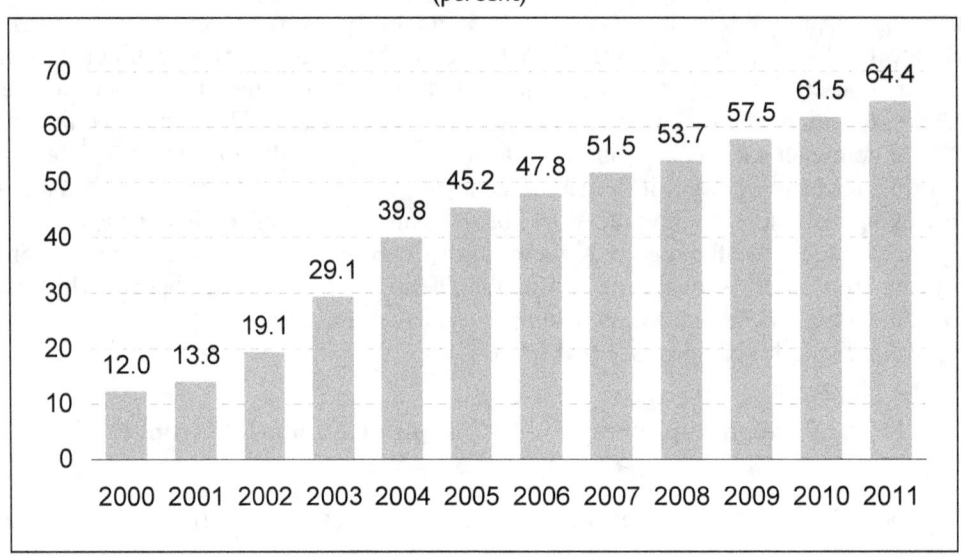

Source: U.S. International Trade Commission DataWeb.

Global Supply Chains, China, and the Apple iPod: Who Benefits?

Many U.S. companies sign contracts with Taiwanese firms to have their products manufactured (mainly in China), and then shipped to the United States where they are sold by U.S. firms under their own brand name. In many instances, the level of value-added that occurs in China (often it simply involves assemblage) can be quite small relative to the overall cost/price of the final product. One study by researchers at the University of California looked at the production of a 2005 Apple 30 gigabyte video iPod, which is made in China by Foxconn, a Taiwanese company, using parts produced globally (mainly in Asia). The study estimated that it cost about $144 to make each iPod unit. Of this amount, only about $4, or 2.8% of the total cost, was attributable to the Chinese workers who assembled it; the rest of the costs were attributable to the numerous firms involved in making the parts (for example, Japanese firms provided the highest-value components—the hard drive and the display).[25] From a trade aspect, U.S. trade data would have recorded the full value of each iPod unit imported from China at $144 (excluding shipping costs) as originating from China, even though the value added in China was quite small. The retail price of the iPod sold in the United States was $299, meaning that there was a mark-up of about $155 per unit, which was attributable to transportation costs, retail and distributor margins, and Apple's profits. The study estimated that Apple earned at least $80 on each unit it sold in its stores, making it the single largest beneficiary (in terms of gross profit) of the sale of the iPod. The study concluded that Apple's innovation in developing and engineering the iPod and its ability to source most of its production to low-cost countries, such as China, has helped enable it to become a highly competitive and profitable firm (as well as a source for high-paying jobs in the United States). The iPod example illustrates that the rapidly changing nature of global supply chains has made it increasing difficult to interpret the implications of U.S. trade data. Such data may show where products are being imported from, but they often fail to reflect who benefits from that trade. Chinese trade data indicate that over 50% of its exports are generated by foreign-invested firms in China. Thus, in many instances, U.S. imports from China are really imports from many countries.

China's Tariff Schedule

China has significantly reduced its tariffs over the past three decades. China's simple average most-favored nation (MFN) applied tariff rate fell from around 50% in the early 1980s, to 15.6% in 2001, and to 9.6% in 2010.[26] However, some U.S. policymakers complain that U.S. exporters to China face much higher tariff rates than do Chinese exporters to the United States. For example, as indicated in **Table 6**, China's simple average MFN applied tariff rate in 2010 was 174% higher than the U.S. rate of 3.5%. Such large differences in tariff rates exist across broad product categories. For example, China's tariff rate on passenger vehicles (25%) was 10 times higher than the U.S. level (2.5%). Imported products into China are also subject to a value-added tax, which ranges from 5% to 17%.[27]

---

[25] Communications of the ACM, *Who Captures Value in a Global Innovation Network? The Case of Apple's iPod*, March 2009.

[26] In comparison, the simple average MFN applied tariff rate for other major emerging markets was as follows: Russia (9.5%), India (13.0%), and Brazil (13.7%).

[27] USTR, *2012 National Trade Estimate of Foreign Trade Barriers*, March 2012, p. 68.

Table 6. Comparison of Chinese and U.S. Simple Average MFN Tariff Rates in 2010

(%)

	China	U.S.
Overall Average Applied MFN Rate	9.6	3.5
Animal products	14.8	2.3
Dairy products	12.0	20.3
Fruit, vegetables, plants	14.8	4.9
Coffee, tea	14.7	3.2
Cereals & preparations	24.3	3.5
Oilseeds, fats & oils	11.0	4.6
Sugars and confectionery	27.4	10.3
Beverages & tobacco	22.3	15.6
Cotton	15.2	4.1
Other agricultural products	11.4	1.1
Fish & fish products	10.9	1.0
Minerals & metals	7.4	1.7
Petroleum	4.8	1.4
Chemicals	6.6	2.8
Wood, paper, etc.	4.4	0.5
Textiles	9.6	7.9
Clothing	16.0	11.7
Leather, footwear, etc.	13.2	3.9
Non-electrical machinery	8.0	1.2
Electrical machinery	8.3	1.7
Transport equipment	11.5	3.0
Passenger Vehicles	25.0	2.5
Other Manufactures	11.9	2.4

Source: WTO World Tariff Profiles, 2011.

Note: Imports into China are also subject to a value-added tax; the standard rate is 17%.

U.S.-China Investment Ties[28]

Investment plays a large and growing role in U.S.-China commercial ties.[29] China's investment in U.S. assets can be broken down into several categories, including holdings of U.S. securities, foreign direct investment (FDI), and other non-bond investments. A significant share of China's investment in the United States is comprised of U.S. securities, while FDI constitutes the bulk of

---

[28] U.S. data on FDI flows to and from China differ from Chinese data on FDI flows to and from the United States. This section examines only U.S. data.

[29] Investment is often a major factor behind trade flows. Firms that invest overseas often import machinery, parts, and other inputs from the parent company to manufacture products for export or sale locally. Other such invested overseas firms may produce inputs and ship them to their parent company for final production.

U.S. investment in China. The Treasury Department defines foreign holdings of U.S. securities as "U.S. securities owned by foreign residents (including banks and other institutions) except where the owner has a direct investment relationship with the U.S. issuer of the securities." U.S. statutes define FDI as "the ownership or control, directly or indirectly, by one foreign resident of 10% or more of the voting securities of an incorporated U.S. business enterprise or the equivalent interest in an unincorporated U.S. business enterprise, including a branch."[30] The U.S. Bureau of Economic Analysis (BEA) reports data on FDI flows to and from the United States.[31] China has also invested in a number of U.S. companies, projects, and various ventures which do meet the U.S. definition of FDI, and thus, are not reflected in BEA's data.

China's Holdings of U.S. Securities[32]

China's holdings of U.S. public and private securities are significant.[33] These include U.S. Treasury securities, U.S. government agency (such as Freddie Mac and Fannie Mae) securities, corporate securities, and equities (such as stocks). U.S. Treasury securities, which help the federal government finance its budget deficit, are the largest category of U.S. securities held by China.[34] As indicated in **Table 7** and **Figure 6**, China's holdings of U.S. Treasury securities increased from $118 billion in 2002 to $1.15 trillion in 2011 (year-end), making China the largest foreign holder of U.S. Treasury securities (it overtook Japan in 2008). China's holdings of U.S. Treasury securities in 2011 were down 0.7% over the previous year. Because of China's capital controls and restrictions on foreign investment in China's equity and bond markets, U.S. holdings of Chinese securities are relatively small compared to U.S. holdings in other countries.[35] U.S. holdings of Chinese securities totaled $102.2 billion in 2010 at year end (98.4% of which were in equities), up from $12.7 billion in 1994 year-end.[36]

China's large holdings of U.S. securities can be largely attributed to its policy of intervening in exchange rate markets to limit the appreciation of its currency, the renminbi (RMB), to the U.S. dollar (discussed in more detail below). For example, the Chinese government requires Chinese exporters (who are often paid in dollars) to turn over their dollars in exchange for RMB. As a result, the Chinese government has accumulated a significant amount of dollars. Rather than

---

[30] 15 CFRS 806.15(a)(1). The 10% ownership share is the threshold considered to represent an effective voice or lasting influence in the management of an enterprise. See BEA, *International Economic Accounts, BEA Series Definitions*, available at http://www.bea.gov/international.

[31] BEA also reports FDI data according to broad industrial sections, including mining; utilities; wholesale trade; information; depository institutions; finance (excluding depository institutions); professional, scientific, and technical services; non-bank holding companies; manufacturing (including food, chemicals, primary and fabricated metals, machinery, computers and electronic products, electrical equipment, appliances and components, transportation equipment, and other manufacturing); and other industries.

[32] For additional information on this issue, see CRS Report RL34314, *China's Holdings of U.S. Securities: Implications for the U.S. Economy*, by Wayne M. Morrison and Marc Labonte.

[33] The Treasury Department estimates that China's total holdings of U.S. government and private securities were $1.7 trillion as of June 2011, of which, 76% ($1.3 trillion) were in U.S. Treasury securities.

[34] Some observers characterize foreign holdings of U.S. Treasury securities as "foreign ownership of U.S. government debt."

[35] China was the 16th-largest market for U.S. holdings of foreign securities. In terms of U.S. investment in foreign equities, China was the 15th-largest market.

[36] U.S. Department of the Treasury, *Report on U.S. Portfolio Holdings of Foreign Securities as of December 31, 2010*, October 2011.

---

holding onto U.S. dollars, which earn no interest, the Chinese government has chosen to invest many of them into U.S. Treasury securities because they are seen as a relatively safe investment.[37]

Table 7. China's Holdings of U.S. Treasury Securities: 2002-2011

	2002	2003	2004	2005	2006	2007	2008	2009	2010	2011
China's Holdings ($ billions)	118.0	159.0	222.9	310.0	396.9	477.6	727.4	894.8	1,160.1	1,151.9
China's Holdings as a Percent of Total Foreign Holdings	9.6%	10.4%	12.1%	15.2%	18.9%	20.3%	23.6%	24.2%	26.1%	23.0%

Source: U.S. Treasury Department, year-end data.

Figure 6. China's Holdings of U.S. Treasury Securities: 2002-2011 (year-end)

($ billions)

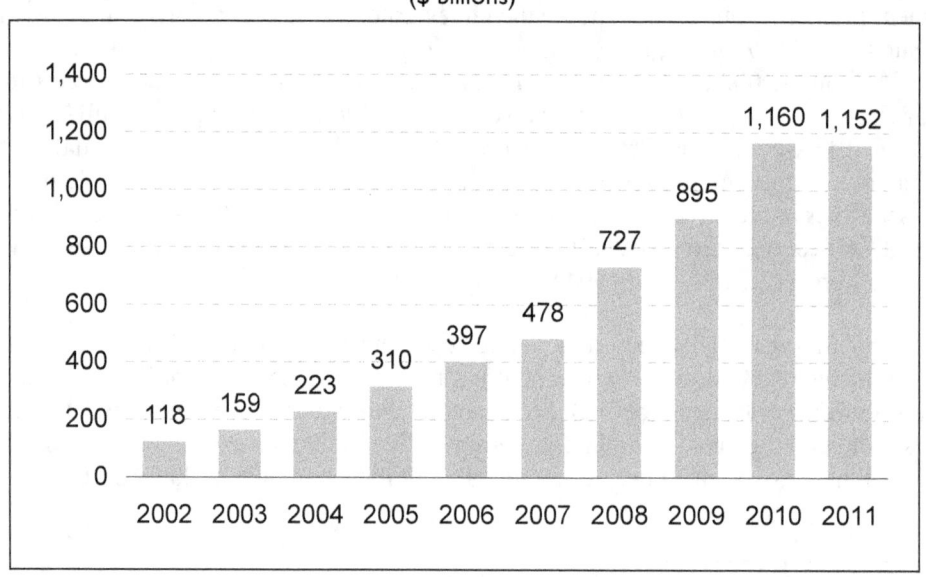

Source: U.S. Department of the Treasury.

Legislation has been introduced in the 112th Congress that would seek to assess the implications for the United States of China's ownership of U.S. debt.

- H.R. 2166 (Sam Johnson) and S. 1028 (Cornyn), both titled "Foreign-Held Debt Transparency and Threat Assessment Act," would seek to increase the transparency of foreign ownership of U.S. debt instruments, especially in regard to China, in order to better assess the potential risks such holdings could pose for the United States. The bills state, for example, that under certain circumstances,

---

[37] However, over the past years, Chinese officials have expressed concern over the "safety" of their large holdings of U.S. debt. They worry that growing U.S. government debt and expansive monetary policies will eventually spark inflation in the United States, resulting in a sharp depreciation of the dollar. This would diminish the value of China's dollar asset holdings.[37] Some Chinese officials have called for replacing the dollar as the world's major reserve currency with some other currency arrangement, such as through the International Monetary Fund's special drawing rights system, although many economists question whether this would be a feasible alternative in the short run.

China's holdings of U.S. debt could give it a tool with which it can try to manipulate U.S. domestic and foreign policymaking, including the U.S. relationship with Taiwan; and that China could attempt to destabilize the U.S. economy by rapidly divesting large portions of its holdings of U.S. debt instruments. The bills would require the President to issue a quarterly report on foreign holders of U.S. debt instruments, which would include a breakdown of foreign ownership by country of domicile and by the type of creditor (i.e., public, quasi-public, private); an analysis of the country's purpose and long-term intentions in regard to its U.S. debt holdings; an analysis of the current and foreseeable risks to U.S. national security and economic stability of each nation's U.S. debt holdings; and a determination whether such risks are "acceptable or unacceptable." If the President determined that a foreign country's holdings of U.S. debt instruments were an unacceptable risk, he would be required to formulate an action plan to reduce that risk.

- H.R. 1540 (McKeon) would, among other things, require the Secretary of Defense to conduct a national security risk assessment of U.S. federal debt held by China.[38] In addition, the Director of the Congressional Budget Office would be required to determine, and make publicly available, the amount of accrued interest on U.S. federal debt paid to China during the past five years.

Some analysts counter that China's holdings of U.S. debt gives it very little practical leverage over the United States. They argue that, given China's economic dependency on a stable and growing U.S. economy, and its substantial holdings of U.S. securities, any attempt to try to sell a large share of those holdings would likely damage both the U.S. and Chinese economies.[39] Such a move could also cause the U.S. dollar to sharply depreciate against global currencies, which could reduce the value of China's remaining holdings of U.S. dollar assets. Analysts also note that, while China is the largest foreign owner of U.S. Treasury Securities, those holdings are equal to only 8% of total U.S. public debt (2010). Finally, it is argued that, as long as China continues to largely peg the RMB to the U.S. dollar, it has little choice but to purchase U.S. dollar assets in order to maintain that peg.

Bilateral Foreign Direct Investment Flows

The level of foreign direct investment (FDI) flows between China and the United States are relatively small given the large volume of trade between the two countries.[40] Many analysts contend that an expansion of bilateral FDI could greatly improve commercial ties.

The U.S. Bureau of Economic Affairs (BEA) reports data on FDI flows to and from the United States.[41] It estimates the cumulative level of Chinese FDI in the United States through the end of 2010 at $3.2 billion on a historical-cost (or book value) basis (see **Table 8**). However, these data

---

[38] The bill, titled the National Defense Authorization Act for Fiscal Year 2012, passed the House on May 26, 2011.

[39] Some analysts counter that the ability of China to possibly disrupt the U.S. economy through selling off U.S. government debt (despite the potential costs to the Chinese economy) puts the United States in a vulnerable position.

[40] Note, U.S. and Chinese data on FDI flows between each other differ.

[41] According the BEA, direct investment implies that a person in one country has a lasting interest in, and a degree of influence over the management of, a business enterprise in another. As such, it defines FDI as ownership or control of 10% or more of an enterprise's voting securities, or the equivalent, is considered evidence of such a lasting interest or degree of influence over management.

---

do not reflect FDI that Chinese investors may have made through offshore locations (such as Hong Kong) to invest in the United States. To reflect this, the BEA attempts to measure the level of FDI inflows according to the country of "ultimate beneficial owner" (UBO). These measurements raise the estimate of China's cumulative FDI flows to the United States through 2010 by 86% to $5.8 billion.[42] The UBO measurement would rank China as the 30th-largest source of total FDI in the United States through 2010. Some analysts contend that the BEA's data on China's FDI in the United States do not fully capture all investments. For example, the Rhodium Group (a private research consultancy and advisory company) estimates cumulative Chinese FDI flows to the United States through the end of 2010 at $11.7 billion and that the amount of new Chinese FDI in the United States in 2010 was $5.2 billion.[43]

U.S. FDI in China is significantly higher than China's FDI in the United States, according to BEA data.[44] Cumulative U.S. FDI in China through 2010 was $60.5 billion, which accounted for nearly 10% of total U.S. FDI in Asia and the Pacific. U.S. FDI flows to China fell by about $7.9 billion in 2009, due largely to the effects of the global economic slowdown, but grew by $9.6 billion in 2010. BEA estimates that U.S. majority-owned non-bank affiliates in China employed 774,000 workers in China in 2008.[45]

Table 8. U.S. Data on Annual U.S.–China Bilateral FDI Flows: 2005-2010 and Cumulative Value of FDI at Year-End 2010

($ millions)

	2005	2006	2007	2008	2009	2010	Cumulative: Value of FDI at 2010 Year-End
China's FDI in the United States	146	315	8	500	35	1,364	3,150
U.S. FDI in China	1,955	4,226	5,243	15,971	-7,853	9,565	60,452

Source: U.S. Bureau of Economic Analysis.

Notes: Cumulative data are on a historical-cost basis. Excludes Chinese FDI in the United States that may have been made through other countries. Using the country of ultimate beneficial owner would raise China's cumulative FDI in the United States through 2010 at $5,845 million.

---

[42] See BEA UBO tables at http://www.bea.gov/international/di1fdibal htm.

[43] They estimate cumulative Chinese FDI in the United States through 2011 at $15.9 billion, and the flow of new FDI to the United States in 2011 at $4.2 billion. See Rhodium Group, *China Investment Monitor, Tracking Chinese Direct Investment in the U.S.* at http://rhgroup net/interactive/china-investment-monitor.

[44] The United States is a relatively large source of FDI in China, ranking fourth in cumulative FDI through 2010.

[45] BEA, *U.S. Direct Investment Abroad: Financial and Operating Data for U.S. Multinational Companies*, available at http://www.bea.gov/international/di1usdop htm.

Chinese Companies in the United States

Although the level of Chinese FDI in the United States is relatively small, many Chinese firms view the United States as a key part of their efforts to become more globally competitive companies, move closer to their U.S. customers, circumvent perceived trade and investment barriers (such as the Buy American Act), and to avoid U.S. trade remedy measures (such as antidumping duties). Some examples of Chinese FDI in the United States include the following:

The Dalian Wanda Group Corporation Ltd. on May 21, 2011, announced that it had signed a merger and acquisition agreement to acquire AMC Entertainment (the world's second-largest theater chain) for $2.6 billion.

Suntech Power Holdings Co., Ltd., the world's largest producer of solar panels, opened a solar plant in Goodyear, AZ, in October 2010, employing 100 workers.

Sany Group, a global producer of construction equipment, founded Sany America Inc. in 2006, headquartered in Peachtree City, GA. In 2007, it announced it would invest $100 million to create and establish a manufacturing facility for constructing and engineering Sany products, with expected employment of 300 workers by the time the project is completed.[46]

Wanxiang Group, an automotive parts manufacturer, established Wanxiang America Corporation in 1994, based in Illinois. Over the past decade, Wangxing America reportedly has purchased or invested in more than 20 U.S. firms and employs 5,000 U.S. workers—more than any other Chinese company.[47]

Pacific Centuries Motor (now a subsidiary of AVIC Automobile Industry Co., Ltd, a state-owned firm) purchased Nexteer Automotive, a Michigan-based firm that producers steering and driveline systems, for an estimated $450 million.[48]

Tianjin Pipe Corporation, China's largest steel pipe-maker, announced in 2009 that it planned to spend $1 billion to construct a mini-mill facility in Gregory, TX, that will manufacture steel products from recycled scrap steel. Over the first 10 years of operation, the project is projected to boost the local economy by $2.7 billion and generate $327 million in direct employee salaries.[49]

Haier Group, a major global appliance and electronics firm, maintains its corporate headquarters for Haier America in New York City, has sales offices in 13 U.S. states, and operates a $40 million refrigerator plant in Camden, SC, reportedly the first U.S. manufacturing facility built by a Chinese firm (2000).

ZTE Corporation, one of China's largest telecommunications manufacturers, established a U.S. presence in 1995. ZTE USA is headquartered in Dallas, TX, and maintains R&D facilities in five U.S. states.

Huawei Technologies is a leading global information and communications technology solutions provider. Since gaining a U.S. presence in 2011, Huawei has reportedly partnered with 280 U.S. technology providers, with total procurement contracts exceeding $30 billion, covering such items as software, components, chipsets, and services. In February, Huawei announced procurement contracts with U.S. firms worth $6 billion.[50]

Golden Dragon Precise Copper Tube Group Inc., (one of the world's largest precise copper tube manufacturers) announced in February 2012 that it planned to build a $100 million manufacturing facility in Alabama.

In addition to China's FDI in the United States and its holdings in U.S. Treasury securities, China (as of June 2011) held $159 billion in U.S. equities (such as stocks), up from $3 billion in June 2005. It also held $241 billion in U.S. agency securities, many of which are asset-backed (such as

---

[46] Sany America website at http://www.sanyamerica.com/about-sany-america.php#ribbon.

[47] Washington Post, "Job creation seen as key to China's investment in U.S," January 19, 2011, available at http://www.washingtonpost.com/wp-dyn/content/article/2011/01/18/AR2011011806676.html.

[48] The purchase reportedly represents China's biggest single investment in the global auto parts-making industry and will make the Chinese company the largest private employer in Saginaw, Michigan at nearly 3,000 (Source: New York Times, *G.M. Sells Parts Maker to a Chinese Company*, November 29, 2010). The firm owns 20 manufacturing plants worldwide, 5 regional engineering and test centers, and 14 local customer support centers.

[49] Xinhua News Agency, "U.S official hails Chinese Project in Texas, October 11, 2011."

[50] http://www.prnewswire.com/news-releases/huawei-poised-to-sustain-tens-of-thousands-of-job-opportunities-for-us-businesses-139525078.html.

Fannie Mae and Freddie Mac securities),[51] and $16 billion in corporate bonds. The China Investment Corporation (CIC), a sovereign wealth fund established by the Chinese government in 2007 with $200 billion in registered capital to help better manage China's foreign exchange reserves, has been one of the largest Chinese purchasers of U.S. equities and other U.S. assets; it has stakes in such firms as Morgan Stanley, the Blackstone Group, and J.C. Flowers & Co.[52] It appears that many of the investments by the CIC and other Chinese entities have attempted to avoid political controversy in the United States by limiting its ownership shares to less than 10%.

Issues Raised by Chinese FDI in the United States

Many U.S. analysts contend that greater Chinese FDI in the United States, especially in "greenfield" projects (new ventures) that manufacture products or provide services in the United States and create new jobs for U.S. workers,[53] could help improve bilateral economic relations and might lessen perceptions among some critics in the United States that growing U.S.-China trade undermines U.S. employment and harms U.S. economic interests.[54] A number of analysts note that China's outward FDI has been growing rapidly since 2004 and is likely to continue in the years ahead.[55] Such analysts contend that greater efforts should be made by U.S. policymakers to encourage Chinese firms to invest in the United States rather than block them for political reasons. In June 2011, President Obama issued an executive order establishing the "SelectUSA Initiative" to coordinate federal efforts to promote and retain investment in the United States. According to a White House factsheet issued during the U.S. visit of Chinese Vice President Xi Jinping in February 2012, China was already one of SwlectUSA top 10 focus markets and that the Administration was planning a significant expansion of the initiative, including with resources dedicated to attracting Chinese investors and facilitating their investment. The two sides further pledged to deepen cooperation on infrastructure financing.[56]

Some critics of China's current FDI policies and practices contend that they are largely focused on mergers and acquisitions that are geared toward boosting the competitive position of Chinese firms and enterprises favored by the Chinese government for development (some of which also may be receiving government subsidies). In some instances, it is argued, such investment is done largely to obtain technology and know-how for Chinese firms, but does little to boost the U.S. economy. Another major issue relating to Chinese FDI in the United States is the relative lack of transparency of Chinese firms, especially in terms of their connections to the central government. Whenever Chinese state-owned enterprises (SOEs) attempt to purchase U.S. company assets, many U.S. analysts begin to ask what role government officials in Beijing played in that decision. Many U.S. policymakers are troubled by the possibility that efforts by Chinese SOEs to acquire U.S. company assets could be part of a Chinese government's strategy to develop global Chinese

---

[51] U.S. Department of the Treasury, *Preliminary Report on Foreign Portfolio Holdings of U.S. Securities at End-June 2011*, February, 29, 2012.

[52] For more information on the CIC, see CRS Report R41441, *China's Sovereign Wealth Fund: Developments and Policy Implications*, by Michael F. Martin.

[53] According to the BEA, Chinese majority-owned nonbank affiliates in the United States employed 1,700 U.S. workers in 2006 (most recent data available).

[54] During the 1980s, Japanese firms significantly boosted their FDI in the United States, such as in automobile manufacturing, in part to help to alleviate bilateral trade tensions.

[55] China reports that its overseas FDI in 2010 was $68.8 billion, ranking it fifth in the world. China's accumulated through 2010 overseas FDI was $317.2 billion.

[56] The White House, *Joint Fact Sheet on Strengthening U.S.-China Economic Relations*, February 14, 2012.

firms that may one day threaten the economic viability of U.S. firms. Chinese officials contend that investment decisions by Chinese companies, including SOEs and publicly held firms (where the government is the largest shareholder), are solely based on commercial considerations, and have criticized U.S. investment policies as "protectionist."

According to the Foreign Investment and National Security Act (FINSA) of 2007 (P.L. 110-149), the Committee on Foreign Investment in the United States (CFIUS) may conduct an investigation on the effect of an investment transaction on national security if the covered transaction is a foreign government-controlled transaction (in addition to if the transaction threatens to impair national security, or results in the control of a critical piece of U.S. infrastructure by a foreign person).[57] The House report on the bill (H.Rept. 110-24, H.R. 556) noted: "The Committee believes that acquisitions by certain government-owned companies do create heightened national security concerns, particularly where government-owned companies make decisions for inherently governmental—as opposed to commercial—reasons."

There have been several instances in which efforts by Chinese firms (oftentimes these have been SOEs or state-favored firms) have raised concerns of some U.S. policymakers and/or U.S. stakeholders:

- In 2004, Lenovo Group Limited, a computer company primarily owned by the Chinese government, signed an agreement with IBM Corporation to purchase IBM's personal computer division for $1.75 billion. Some U.S. officials raised national security concerns over potential espionage activities that could occur in the United States at IBM research facilities by Lenovo employees if the deal went through. A review of the agreement by CFIUS took place in which IBM and Lenovo were able to address certain national security concerns and, as a result, the acquisition was completed in April 2005.[58]

- In 2005, the China National Offshore Oil Corporation (CNOOC), a Chinese SOE, made a bid to buy UNOCAL, a U.S. energy company, for $18.5 billion, but widespread opposition in Congress led CNOOC to withdraw its bid. Some Members argued at the time that the proposed takeover represented a clear threat to the energy and national security of the United States, would put vital oil assets in the Gulf of Mexico and Alaska into the hands of a Chinese state-controlled company, could transfer a host of highly advanced technologies to China, and that CNOOC's bid to take over UNOCAL would be heavily subsidized by the Chinese government. Some Members argued that "vital" U.S. energy assets should never sold to the Chinese government. CNOOC officials referred to U.S. political opposition to the sale as "regrettable and unjustified."[59]

---

[57] CFIUS is an interagency committee that serves the President in overseeing the national security implications of foreign investment in the U.S. economy. See CRS Report RL33388, *The Committee on Foreign Investment in the United States (CFIUS)*, by James K. Jackson.

[58] IBM and Lenovo reportedly agreed to address national security concerns by CFIUS. For example, it was agreed that 1,900 employees from a North Carolina research facility, which IBM had shared with other technology companies, would move to another building. See the *Financial Times*, "US State Department limits use of Chinese PCs," May 18, 2006.

[59] The Senate report of its version of FINSA (S.Rept. 110-80, S. 1610) noted that CNOOC's attempt to acquire UNOCAL "led many members of Congress to raise questions about the transfer of ownership or control of certain sectors of the U.S. economy to foreign companies, especially to foreign companies located within or controlled by countries the governments of which might not be sympathetic to U.S. regional security interests."

- In September 2007, Huawei announced plans, along with its partner, Bain Capital Partners, to buy the U.S. firm 3Com Corporation, a provider of data networking equipment, for $2.2 billion. However, the proposed merger was withdrawn in February 2008 following a review of the deal by CFIUS when Huawei and its partner failed to adequately address U.S. national security concerns raised by CFIUS members.[60]

- In July 2009, China's Northwest Nonferrous International Investment Company, a Chinese SOE, made a $26 million offer to purchase a 51% stake in the Firstgold Corporation, a U.S. exploration-stage company. However, the deal reportedly raised national concerns within CFUIS because some of the mines controlled by Firstgold were near U.S. military installations. As a result, the Chinese firm withdrew its bid in December 2009.[61]

- In February 2010, Emcore Corporatation, a provider of compound semiconductor-based components, subsystems, and systems for the fiber optics and solar power markets, announced it had agreed to sell 60% interest in its fiber optics business (excluding its satellite communications and specialty photonics fiber optics businesses) to China's Tangshan Caofeidian Investment Corporation (TCIC) for $27.8 million. However, Emcore announced in June 2010 that the deal had been ended because of concerns by CFIUS.[62]

- In May 2010, Anshan Iron and Steel Group Corporation (Ansteel), a major Chinese state-owned steel producer, announced plans to form a joint venture with Steel Development Company, a U.S. firm in Mississippi, to build and operate four mills to produce reinforcing bar and other bar products used in infrastructure applications, and one mill that would be capable of producing electrical and silicon grades of steel used in energy applications.[63] In July 2010, the Congressional Steel Caucus sent a letter signed by 50 Members to Secretary of the Treasury Tim Geithner, expressing concerns over the effect the investment would have "on American jobs and our national security."[64] At a February 2012 hearing on China's SOEs, Representative Visclosky, chairman of the Congressional Steel Caucus stated: "As a Caucus, we were concerned that the investment would allow a Chinese state-owned enterprise to pursue the government of China's aims, and not the aims of the employer, the American worker, or the market. We were concerned that this investment would allow the full force and financing of the Chinese government to exploit the American steel market from American soil. We also were concerned that China would have access to new steel production technologies and information regarding American national security infrastructure projects."[65]

---

[60] Although Huawei states that it is a private company wholly owned by its employees, many analysts contend that the company has close connections to the Chinese military. In addition, Huawei has also reportedly received extensive financial support from the Chinese government, including a $30 billion line of credit from China Development Bank.

[61] *New York Times*, "Chinese Withdraw Offer for Nevada Gold Concern," December 21, 2009.

[62] Emcore Press Release, June 28, 2010, available at http://www.emcore.com/news_events/release?y=2010&news=249.

[63] A press release by Ansteel stated that its intensions are "to capitalize on the opportunity to enter into an overseas joint venture with a company that is focused on utilizing advanced technology in an environmentally friendly and highly profitable manner." See, http://www.steeldevelopment.com/documents/ansteel2010.pdf.

[64] See letter at http://visclosky house.gov/SC_Geithner_CFIUS_7.2.10.pdf.

[65] Testimony of Congressman Peter J. Visclosky before the U.S.-China Economic and Security Review Commission on (continued...)

- In May 2010, Huawei bought certain intellectual property assets of 3Leaf Systems (an insolvent U.S. technology firm) for $2 million. A February 2011 letter issued by Senators Jim Webb and Jon Kyl to Commerce Secretary Gary Locke and Treasury Secretary Tim Geithner stated: "We are convinced that any attempt Huawei makes to expand its presence in the U.S. or acquire U.S. companies warrants thorough scrutiny. Moreover, the 3Leaf acquisition appears certain to generate transfer to China by Huawei of advanced U.S. computing technology. Allowing Huawei and, by extension, communist China to have access to this core technology could pose a serious risk as U.S. computer networks come to further rely on and integrate this technology."[66] In February 2011, Huawei stated that it been formally notified by CFIUS that it should withdraw its application to acquire 3Leaf's assets, which it later did.[67] In an "Open Letter," Huawei invited the U.S. government to carry out a formal investigation on any concerns it may have about Huawei.[68]

- On May 9, 2012, the Federal Reserve announced that it had approved (1) the application by Industrial and Commercial Bank of China Limited, China Investment Corporation, and Central Huijin Investment Ltd., to become bank holding companies by acquiring up to 80% of the voting shares of the Bank of East Asia (USA) National Association; (2) the Bank of China's application to establish a branch in Chicago, IL; and (3) the application by the Agricultural Bank of China Limited to establish a state-licensed branch in New York City.[69] In a letter to Federal Reserve Chairman Ben Bernanke, Senator Robert Casey noted that each of entities approved by the Federal Reserve was state-owned, and he expressed concern that "these banks and their U.S. subsidiaries will use their state-support as a way to underprice U.S. banks that abide by U.S. law and do not have the support of a sovereign country behind them."[70]

Chinese Restrictions on U.S. FDI in China

U.S. trade officials have urged China to liberalize its FDI regime in order to boost U.S. business opportunities in, and expand U.S. exports to China. Although China is one of the world's top recipients of FDI, the Chinese central government imposes numerous restrictions on the level and of types of FDI allowed in China. To a great extent, China's investment policies appear to be linked to industrial policies that seek to promote the development of sectors identified by the government as critical to future economic development. For example, since the early 1980s, the Chinese government has encouraged foreign auto companies to invest in China, but has limited

---

(...continued)

China's State-Owned and State-Controlled Enterprises, February 15, 2012.

[66] The letter also raised concerns over allegations that Huawei had ties to the Iranian government, had received substantial subsidies from the Chinese government, and had a poor record of protecting intellectual property rights.

[67] Huawei initially stated that it would decline CFIUS's recommendation with the intent of going through all of the procedures of the CFIUS process (including a potential decision by the President) in order to "reveal the truth about Huawei."

[68] Huawei, Open Letter, February 25, 2011, available at http://www.huawei.com/huawei_open_letter.do.

[69] Senator Robert Casey, *Press Release*, May 10, 2012, available at http://www federalreserve.gov.

[70] The letter is available at http://www.casey.senate.gov/newsroom/press/release/?id=b940fb00-0a69-42d6-bcff-6ac72c8ce0c1.

FDI in that sector to 50-50 joint ventures with domestic Chinese partners.[71] In addition, the central government maintains a "Guideline Catalogue for Foreign Investment" (the latest revision was issued in January 2012), which lists FDI categories that are encouraged, restricted, or prohibited.[72] Many of the sectors under the "encouraged" category include high technology, green technology, and energy conservation, and pollution control.[73] Several of the sectors under the "restricted" category limit FDI to joint ventures (such as for rare earth smelting) or where the Chinese parties are the controlling shareholders (such as railway passenger transport companies). "Prohibited" sectors are those that fall under "national security" concerns (such as manufacturing of ammunition and weapons) or are categories where the government seeks to preserve state monopolies (such as postal companies) or protect Chinese firms from foreign competition (such as mining of rare earth elements).

The Chinese government also sets restrictions on FDI inflows during the investment screening process, or through its mergers and acquisition regulations, especially when seeking to protect pillar or strategic industries that the central government (as well as many provincial and local governments) seeks to promote. Many critics of China's investment policies contend that the Chinese government often requires foreign firms to transfer technology to their China partners, and sometimes to set up research and development facilities in China, in exchange for access to China's markets.[74] Foreign-invested firms in China face a number of challenges, including local protectionism, lack of regulatory transparency, IPR theft, and discriminatory license practices.

The United States and China have held negotiations on reaching a bilateral investment treaty (BIT) with the goal of expanding bilateral investment opportunities. U.S. negotiators hope such a treaty would improve the investment climate for U.S. firms in China by enhancing legal protections and dispute resolution procedures, and by obtaining a commitment from the Chinese government that it would treat U.S. investors no less favorably than Chinese investors. However, some groups have argued that a BIT with China could hurt U.S. workers by encouraging more U.S. firms to relocate to China.[75]

In April 2012, the Obama Administration released a "Model Bilateral Investment Treaty" that was developed to enhance U.S. objectives in the negotiation of new BITs.[76] The new BIT model establishes mechanisms to promote greater transparency, labor and environment requirements, disciplines to prevent parties from imposing domestic technology requirements, and measures to boost the ability of investors to participate in the development of standards and technical regulations on a nondiscriminatory basis.

---

[71] The automotive industry was designated a "pillar industry" by the Chinese government in 1991.

[72] China also maintains a permitted category which represents a neutral position by the government that FDI is neither encouraged or discouraged. Prior to 2012, FDI in the manufacture of complete automobiles was listed as an encouraged category.

[73] One major function of the Guideline Catalogue for Foreign Investment is to promote FDI in sectors that the government has targeted for growth in its five-year macro-economic plans.

[74] USTR, 2011 *Report to Congress On China's WTO Compliance*, December 2011, p.7.

[75] *Inside U.S.-China Trade*, April 28, 2010.

[76] The Administration began efforts to review and revise the U.S. BIT model in 2009. The previous BIT model dated to 2004. The Administration's review process likely meant that negotiations with China for a BIT were someone limited.

Major U.S.-China Trade Issues

China's economic reforms and rapid economic growth, along with the effects of globalization, have caused the economies of the United States and China to become increasingly integrated.[77] Although growing U.S.-China economic ties are considered by most analysts to be mutually beneficial overall, tensions have risen over a number of Chinese economic and trade policies that many U.S. critics charge are protectionist, economically distortive, and damaging to U.S. economic interests. A 2012 survey by the American Chamber of Commerce in China (AmCham China) of its members in China illustrates the complex nature of the bilateral trade relationship. The survey found that 76% of respondents said that they made a profit in China in 2011, and 86% said they would boost investment in their Chinese operations in 2012. However, 37% of respondents stated that it has become more difficult to obtain business licenses in recent years and 51% said license requirements put them at a competitive disadvantage vis-a-vis domestic Chinese firms.[78] According to the USTR, most U.S. trade disputes with China stem from the consequences of its incomplete transition to a free market economy. Major areas of concern for U.S. stakeholders include

- China's web of industrial policies that seek to promote and protect domestic sectors and firms, especially SOEs, deemed by the government to be critical to the country's future economic growth;

- its failure to provide adequate protection of U.S. intellectual property rights (IPR);

- its mixed record on implementing its obligations in the World Trade Organization (WTO) and its failure to join the WTO's Government Procurement Agreement (GPA); and

- its managed currency policy in which the government intervenes to limit the appreciation of the renminbi (RMB) against the dollar and other major currencies in order to make China's export industries more globally competitive.

Chinese "State Capitalism"

Currently, a significant share of China's economy is thought to be driven by market forces. According to a 2010 WTO report, the private sector now accounts for more than 60% of China's gross domestic product (GDP).[79] However, the Chinese government continues to play a major role in economic decision-making. For example, at the macroeconomic level, the Chinese government maintains policies that induce households to save a high level of their income, much

---

[77] The impact of globalization has been a controversial topic in the United States. Some argue that it has made it easier for U.S. firms to shift production overseas, resulting in lost jobs in the United States (especially in manufacturing) and lower wages for U.S. workers. Others contend that globalization has induced U.S. firms to become more efficient and to focus a greater share of their domestic manufacturing on higher-end or more technologically advanced production (while sourcing lower-end production abroad), making such firms more globally competitive. The result has been that the United States continues to be a major global manufacturer in terms of value-added, but there are fewer U.S. workers in manufacturing.

[78] AmCham China. 2012 China Business Climate Survey Report, March 2012, available at http://www.amchamchina.org/businessclimate2012.

[79] World Trade Organization, *Trade Policy Review Body, Trade Policy Review, Report by the Secretariat, China*, Revision, 2010, Part 2, p.1.

---

of which is deposited in state-controlled Chinese banks. This enables the government to provide low-cost financing to Chinese firms, especially SOEs. At the microeconomic level, the Chinese government (at the central and local government level) seeks to promote the development of industries that are deemed critical to the country's future economic development by using various policies, such as subsidies, tax breaks, preferential loans, trade barriers, FDI restrictions, discriminatory regulations and standards, export restrictions on raw materials (such as rare earths) technology transfer requirements imposed on foreign firms, public procurement rules that give preferences to domestic firms, and weak enforcement of IPR laws.

Many analysts contend that the Chinese government's intervention in various sectors through industrial policies has intensified in recent years. The December 2011 U.S. Trade Representative's (USTR's) report on China's WTO trade compliance states that since 2006 there has been a "troubling trend in China toward intensified state intervention" and that China seems to be "embracing state capitalism more strongly."[80]

China's Plan to Modernize the Economy and Promote Indigenous Innovation

Many of the industrial policies that China has implemented or formulated since 2006 appear to stem largely from a comprehensive document issued by China's State Council (the highest executive organ of state power) in 1996 titled the *National Medium-and Long-Term Program for Science and Technology Development (2006-2020)*, often referred to as the MLP. The MLP appears to represent an ambitious plan to modernize the structure of China's economy by transforming it from a global center of low-tech manufacturing to a major center of innovation (by the year 2020) and a global innovation leader by 2050.[81] It also seeks to sharply reduce the country's dependence on foreign technology. The MLP includes the stated goals of "indigenous innovation, leapfrogging in priority fields, enabling development, and leading the future."[82] Some of the broad goals of the MLP state that by 2020:

- The progress of science and technology will contribute 60% or above to China's development.

- The country's reliance on foreign technology will decline to 30% or below (from an estimated current level of 50%).

- Gross expenditures for research and development (R&D) would rise to 2.5% of gross domestic product (from 1.3% in 2005). Priority areas for increased R&D include space programs, aerospace development and manufacturing, renewable energy, computer science, and life sciences.[83]

The document states that "China must place the strengthening of indigenous innovative capability at the core of economic restructuring, growth model change, and national competitiveness enhancement. Building an innovation-oriented country is therefore a major strategic choice for

---

[80] U.S. Trade Representative, *2011 USTR Report to Congress on China's WTO Compliance,* December 2011, p.2.

[81] As some observers describe it, China wants to go from a model of "made in China" to "innovated in China."

[82] The MLP identifies main areas and priority topics, including energy, water and mineral resources, the environment, agriculture, manufacturing, communications and transport, information industry and modern service industries, population and health, urbanization and urban development, public security, and national defense. The report also identifies 16 major special projects and 8 "pioneer technologies."

[83] *R&D Magazine*, December 22, 2009.

China's future development." This goal, according to the document, is to be achieved by formulating and implementing regulations in the country's government procurement law to "encourage and protect indigenous innovation," establishing a coordination mechanism for government procurement of indigenous innovative products, requiring a first-buy policy for major domestically made high-tech equipment and products that possess proprietary intellectual property rights, providing policy support to enterprises in procuring domestic high-tech equipment, and developing "relevant technology standards" through government procurement.

Reaction by U.S. Stakeholders

Beginning in 2009, several U.S. companies began to raise concerns over a number of Chinese government circulars that would establish an "Indigenous Innovation Product Accreditation" system. For example, in November 2009, the Chinese government released a "Circular on Launching the 2009 National Indigenous Innovation Product Accreditation Work," requiring companies to file applications by December 2009 for their products to be considered for accreditation as "indigenous innovation products." U.S. business representatives expressed deep concern over the circulars, arguing that they were protectionist in nature because they extended preferential treatment for Chinese government procurement to domestic Chinese firms that developed and owned intellectual property (IP) and thus largely excluded foreign firms.[84] AmCham China described China's attempt to link IP ownership with market access as "unprecedented worldwide."[85] A letter written by the U.S. Chamber of Commerce and 33 business associations to the Chinese government on December 10, 2009, stated that the indigenous innovations circulars would "make it virtually impossible for any non-Chinese companies to participate in China's government procurement market—even those that have made substantial and long-term investments in China, employ Chinese citizens, and pay taxes to the Chinese government."[86] Such groups contend that a large share of their technology is developed globally and thus it would be difficult to attribute the share of technology developed in China needed to obtain accreditation.[87]

A 2011 AmCham China survey found that 40% of respondents believed that China's indigenous innovation policies would hurt their businesses and 26% said their businesses were already being hurt by such policies.[88] At a November 2011 WTO review of China's IPR policies, the U.S. WTO representative stated that China's policies of adopting indigenous innovation had "created a troubling trend toward increased discriminatory policies which were aimed at coercing technology transfer." He stated that "Chinese regulations, rules and other regulatory measures frequently called for technology transfer, and in certain cases, conditioned, or proposed to

---

[84] U.S. business representatives also claim that the Chinese government is using tax incentives, standards setting and requirements, security regulations, subsidies, technology transfer requirements, and other measures to promote the goals of indigenous innovation.

[85] AmCham China, *2011 White Paper*, April 26, 2011, p. 66.

[86] A copy of the letter can be found at http://online.wsj.com/public/resources/documents/chinaprocurementletter1210.pdf.

[87] Some U.S. business representatives argue that one of the main goals of China's indigenous innovation regulations is to induce foreign firms to boost their R&D activities in China in order to qualify for government contracts.

[88] However 68% of the respondents stated that they were unaffected by indigenous innovation policies and 6% said they had benefited. See AmCham China, 2011 *China Business Climate Survey*.

condition, the eligibility for government benefits or preferences on intellectual property being owned or developed in China, or being licensed, in some cases exclusively, to a Chinese party."[89]

China's Response to U.S. Concerns

The Chinese government responded to U.S. concerns over its indigenous innovation policies by arguing that they did not discriminate against foreign firms or violate global trade rules.[90] However, during the visit of Chinese President Hu Jianto to the United States in January 2011, the Chinese government stated that it would not link its innovation policies to the provision of government procurement preferences.[91] During the May 2011 session of the U.S.-China Strategic and Economic Dialogue (S&ED), China pledged that it would eliminate all of its indigenous innovation products catalogs.[92] During the November 2011 talks held under the U.S.-China Joint Commission on Commerce and Trade (JCCT), the Chinese government announced that the State Council had issued a measure requiring governments of provinces, municipalities, and autonomous regions to eliminate by December 1, 2011, any catalogues or other measures linking innovation policies to government procurement preferences.[93] This occurred after foreign business groups raised concerns that discriminatory indigenous innovation policies might continue to be implemented at the local level even after Hu Jintao's commitment.[94]

Remaining U.S. Concerns

While many U.S. business leaders have applauded China's pledge to delink indigenous innovation from government procurement, some remain wary that China will implement new policies that attempt to provide preferences to local Chinese firms over foreign firms. According to Adam Segal with the Council of Foreign Relations: "Even if China reverses certain policies under U.S. pressure, it will remain dedicated to those goals. U.S. policy is likely to become a game of Whac-a-Mole, beating down one Chinese initiative on indigenous innovation only to see another pop up."[95] U.S. business groups are also concerned with how the MLP blueprint will affect China's commitment to enforcing foreign IPR. They note, for example, that the MLP states: "Indigenous innovation refers to enhancing original innovation, integrated innovation, and re-innovation based on assimilation and absorption of imported technology, in order to improve our

---

[89] Transitional Review Under Section 18 of the Protocol on the Accession of the People's Republic of China, Report to the General Council by the Chair, November 17, 2011, p.4.

[90] Wall Street Journal, *China Defends Rule On 'Indigenous' Tech*, December 15, 2009.

[91] The White House, *U.S. - China Joint Statement*, January 19, 2011.

[92] According to a U.S. fact sheet on the meeting "China pledged to eliminate all of its government procurement indigenous innovation products catalogues and revise Article 9 of the draft Government Procurement Law Implementing Regulations (which have preferences in government procurement to national indigenous innovation products), in fulfillment of President Hu's January 2011 commitment not to link Chinese innovation policies to government procurement preferences. See U.S. Department of the Treasury, The 2011 U.S.-China Strategic and Economic Dialogue U.S. Fact Sheet – Economic Track, May 10, 2011.

[93] U.S. Department of Commerce, *22nd U.S.-China Joint Commission on Commerce and Trade Fact Sheet*, November 21, 2011.

[94] The U.S.-China Business Council reported in February 2011 that it had identified 22 municipal and provincial governments that had issued at least 61 indigenous innovation catalogues. U.S. business representatives sought to ensure that Beijing's pledge on indigenous innovation would apply at all levels of government in China. See U.S.-China Business Council, *Provincial and Local Government Indigenous Innovation Catalogues*, February 2011.

[95] Foreign Affairs, *China's Innovation Wall: Beijing's Push for Homegrown Technology*, September 28, 2010.

---

national innovation capability." To some, this seems to indicate that China intends to take existing technology, make some changes and improvements on it, and then claim it as its own without acknowledging or compensating the original IPR holders. A 2011 report by the U.S. Chamber of Commerce stated that China's indigenous innovation policies led many international technology companies to conclude that the MLP is a "blueprint for technology theft on a scale the world has never seen before."[96]

U.S. officials have attempted to convince Beijing that, while its desire to increase innovation in China is a commendable goal, its efforts to limit the participation of foreign firms in such efforts, or attempting to condition market access in China to the development of IPR by foreign firms in China will hinder, not promote, the advancement of innovation in China. The direction China takes on this issue could have a significant impact on U.S. economic interests as noted by a study by the U.S. International Trade Commission (USITC):

> To the extent that China's policies succeed in accelerating technological progress, productivity, and innovation in the Chinese economy, they could provide spillover benefits for other countries. But if indigenous innovation policies act as a form of technological import substitution, systematically favoring Chinese domestic firms over foreign firms in relevant industries, they would be expected to have a negative effect on foreign firms and economies roughly analogous to what would occur if China simply imposed a protective tariff on imports of goods in the relevant sectors or levied a discriminatory excise tax on the sales of FIEs in the Chinese market.[97]

Intellectual Property Rights (IPR)

U.S. business and government representatives have voiced growing concern over economic losses suffered by U.S. firms as a result of IPR infringement in China (and elsewhere), including those that have resulted from cyber attacks. U.S. innovation and the intellectual property that is generated by such activities have been cited by various economists as a critical source of U.S. economic growth and global competitiveness.[98] For example, according to the Department of Commerce, in 2010, U.S. IP-intensive industries supported at least 40 million jobs and contributed $5.1 trillion (or 34.8%) to U.S. gross domestic product (GDP). A study by NDP Consulting estimated that in 2008, workers in IP-intensive production earned 60% more than workers at similar levels in non-IP industries.[99] A study on the Apple iPod concluded that Apple's innovation in developing and engineering the iPod and its ability to source most of its production to low-cost countries, such as China, have helped enable it to become a highly competitive and profitable firm as well as a creator of high-paying jobs (such as engineers engaged in the design of Apple products) in the United States.[100]

---

[96] U.S. Chamber of Commerce, *China's Drive for 'Indigenous Innovation' - A Web of Industrial Policies*, February 2011, p.4.

[97] USITC, China: Intellectual Property Infringement, Indigenous Innovation Policies, and Frameworks for Measuring the Effects on the U.S. Economy (Investigation No. 332-514, USITC Publication 4199, November 2010, p.6-7.

[98] See CRS Report RL34292, *Intellectual Property Rights and International Trade*, by Shayerah Ilias and Ian F. Fergusson.

[99] Nam Pham, *The Impact of Innovation and the Role of Intellectual Property Rights on U.S. Productivity, Competitiveness, Jobs, Wages and Exports*, 2010, NDP Consulting.

[100] Communications of the ACM, *Who Captures Value in a Global Innovation Network? The Case of Apple's iPod*, March 2009.

Lack of effective and consistent protection of IPR has been cited by U.S. firms as one of the most significant problems they face in doing business in China. Other U.S. firms have expressed concern over pressures they often face from Chinese government entities to share technology and IPR with a Chinese partner. Although China has significantly improved its IPR protection regime over the past few years, U.S. IP industries complain that piracy rates in China continue to remain unacceptably high and economic losses are significant, as illustrated by studies and estimates made by several stakeholders:

- A 2012 AmCham China survey found that 79% of respondents in 2012 felt that China's IPR enforcement was ineffective.[101]

- The USITC estimated that U.S. intellectual property-intensive firms that conducted business in China lost $48.2 billion in sales, royalties, and license fees in 2009 because of IPR violations in China. It also estimated that an effective IPR enforcement regime in China that was comparable to U.S. levels, could increase employment by IP-intensive firms in the United States by 923,000 jobs[102]

- The Business Software Alliance (BSA) estimates the commercial value of illegally used software in China at $7.8 billion in 2010 and that the software piracy rate in China was 78%.[103]

- The U.S. Customs and Border Protection reported that China accounted for 62% of pirated goods seized by the agency in FY2011 (based on domestic value).[104] The value of seized goods originating from China was $110 million.[105]

Chinese officials contend that they have significantly improved their IPR protection regime, but argue that the country lacks the resources and a sophisticated legal system to effectively deal with IPR violations. They also contend that IPR infringement is a serious problem for domestic Chinese firms as well. However, some analysts contend that China's relatively poor record on IPR enforcement can be partially explained by the fact that Chinese leaders want to make China a major producer of capital-intensive and high-technology products, and thus, they are tolerant of IPR piracy if it helps Chinese firms become more technologically advanced. According to an official at the U.S. Chamber of Commerce:

> The newer and emerging challenge to U.S. IPR is not a function of China's lack of political will to crackdown on infringers. Rather, it is a manifestation of a coherent, and government-directed, or at least government-motivated, strategy to lessen China's perceived reliance on foreign innovations and IP. China is actively working to create a legal environment that enables it to intervene in the market for IP, help its own companies to "re-innovate" competing IPR as a substitute to American and other foreign technologies, and potentially

---

[101] AmCham China, *2012 China Business Climate Survey Report*, March 2012, available at http://www.amchamchina.org/businessclimate2012.

[102] The United States International Trade Commission, *China: Effects of Intellectual Property Infringement and Indigenous Innovation Policies on the U.S. Economy*, USITC Publication 4226, May 2011, p. xiv.

[103] BSA, *Eighth Annual Global Software Piracy Study*, May 2011, available at http://portal.bsa.org/globalpiracy2010/downloads/study_pdf/2010_BSA_Piracy_Study-Standard.pdf.

[104] This rate goes up to 80% if seizures of goods from Hong Kong is included.

[105] U.S. Customs and Border Protection, *Intellectual Property Rights, Fiscal Year 2011 Seizure Statistics*, February 2012, available at http://www.cbp.gov/linkhandler/cgov/trade/priority_trade/ipr/ipr_communications/seizure/ipr_seizures_fy2011.ctt/ipr_seizure_fy2011.pdf.

misappropriate U.S. and other foreign IP as components of its industrial policies and internal market regulation.... The common themes throughout these policies are: 1) undermine and displace foreign IP; 2) leverage China's large domestic market to development national champions and promote its own IP, displacing foreign competitors in China; and 3) building on China's domestic successes by displacing competitors in foreign markets.[106]

A recent illustration of alleged IPR theft in China involves American Superconductor Corporation (AMSC). On September 14, 2011, AMSC announced that it was filing criminal and civil complaints in China against Sinovel Wind Group Co. Ltd. (Sinovel), China's largest wind turbine producer, and other parties, alleging the illegal use of AMSC's intellectual property. According to an AMSC press release, Sinovel illegally obtained and used AMSC's wind turbine control software code to upgrade its 1.5 megawatt wind turbines in the field to meet proposed Chinese grid codes and to potentially allow for the use of core electrical components from other manufacturers.[107] In addition, AMSC claimed that Sinovel had refused to pay for past shipments from AMSC and was now refusing to honor contracts for future shipments of components and spare parts as well.[108] According to a specialist in intellectual property at Tufts University, "Chinese companies, once they acquire the needed technology, will often abandon their Western partners on the pretext the technology or product failed to meet Chinese governmental regulations. This is yet another example of a Chinese industrial policy aimed at procuring, by virtually any means, technology in order to provide Chinese domestic industries with a competitive advantage."[109]

During the December 2010 U.S.-China Joint Commission on Commerce and Trade (JCCT),[110] the Chinese government announced several new initiatives to improve its IPR protection regime, including boosting purchases of legitimate software by government agencies and 30 large SOEs. The USTR's 2011 Special 301 report noted that China had launched the "Program for Special Campaign on Combating IPR Infringement and Manufacture and Sales of Counterfeiting and Shoddy Commodities" (Special Campaign) in October 2010, aimed at a broad range of IPR violations. The Special Campaign involved 26 member agencies (led by a Chinese vice premier), and reportedly led to improved government coordination of IPR enforcement by the Chinese government.

The USTR's 2012 Special 301 report stated that, while China had made some notable improvements to its IPR enforcement regime (in particular by making the Special Campaign on IPR enforcement permanent), serious problems remain. These include very high levels of trademark counterfeiting and copyright piracy, the persistence of "notorious" physical and online markets selling IPR-infringing goods, the manufacturing and sale of counterfeit pharmaceuticals, export of counterfeit goods, and discriminatory policies seeking to promote indigenous innovation in China by coercing foreign firms to transfer IPR to Chinese domestic firms. The USTR further noted a "recent alarming increase" in thefts of trade secrets (both in China and outside China) for the benefit of Chinese entities. Many of these problems, according to the

---

[106] Testimony of Jeremie Waterman, Senior Director, Greater China, U.S. Chamber of Commerce, before the U.S. International Trade Commission, *Hearing on China: Intellectual Property Infringement, Indigenous Innovation Policies, and Frameworks for Measuring the Effects on the U.S. Economy*, June 15, 2010.

[107] AMSC claims Sinovel had obtained the intellectual property from a former AMSC employee who was now under arrest in Austria for economic espionage and fraudulent manipulation of data.

[108] AMSC Press Release, "AMSC Filing Criminal and Civil Complaints Against Sinovel," September 14, 2011.

[109] "Data Theft Case May Test U.S. China Ties," *Boston Globe*, September 19, 2011.

[110] The JCCT was established in 1983 to serve as a forum for high-level dialogue on major bilateral trade issues.

USTR, stemmed from the lack of an effective government deterrent to such activities. In addition, while China's campaign to require central and provincial governments to use legitimate software produced a "modest increase" in U.S. software to the Chinese government, piracy rates by Chinese SOEs remained high.[111]

Market access in China remains a significant problem for many U.S. IP industries (such as music and films) and is considered to be a significant cause of high IPR piracy rates. For example, until recently, China limited imports of foreign films to 20 per year. During the visit to the United States by Chinese Vice President Xi Jinping (February 13-17, 2012), China agreed that it would allow more American exports to China of 3D, IMAX, and similar enhanced format movies on favorable commercial terms; strengthen the opportunities to distribute films through private enterprises rather than the state film monopoly; and ensure fairer compensation levels for U.S. blockbuster films distributed by Chinese SOEs.[112]

In the 112th Congress, H.R. 3375 (Steve King) would direct the President to impose duties on imports from China equivalent to the estimated annual loss of revenue to U.S. IPR holders resulted from IPR infringement in China. (The United States has challenged China's IPR policies in the WTO, which are discussed later in the report.)

Technology Transfer Issues

When China entered the WTO in 2011, it agreed that foreign firms would not be pressured by government entities to transfer technology to a Chinese partner as part of the cost of doing business in China. However, many U.S. firms argue that this is a common Chinese practice, although this is difficult to quantify because, oftentimes, U.S. business representatives appear to try to avoid negative publicity regarding the difficulties they encounter doing business in China out of concern over retaliation by the Chinese government.[113]

In 2011, U.S. Treasury Secretary Timothy Geithner charged that "we're seeing China continue to be very, very aggressive in a strategy they started several decades ago, which goes like this: you want to sell to our country, we want you to come produce here. If you want to come produce here, you need to transfer your technology to us."[114] The 2012 survey by AmCham China reported that 33% of its respondents stated that technology transfer requirements were negatively affecting their businesses.[115] A 2010 study by the U.S. Chamber of Commerce stated that growing pressure on foreign firms to share technology in exchange for market access in China was forcing such firms to "anguish over balancing today's profits with tomorrow's survival."[116]

---

[111] USTR, *2012 Special 301 Report*, April 2012, available at
http://www.ustr.gov/sites/default/files/2012%20Special%20301%20Report_0.pdf.

[112] The White House, *Press Release*, February 17, 2012, at http://www.whitehouse.gov/the-press-office/2012/02/17/united-states-achieves-breakthrough-movies-dispute-china.

[113] China denies that public officials exert such pressure and that any technology transfers that do occur in China are the result of commercial agreements between companies.

[114] Reuters, September 23, 2011.

[115] AmCham China, *2012 China Business Climate Survey Report*, March 2012, available at
http://www.amchamchina.org/businessclimate2012

[116] U.S. Chamber of Commerce, *China's Drive for 'Indigenous Innovation' - A Web of Industrial Policies,* July 29, 2010.

However, a 2011 survey by the U.S.-China Business Council found that technology transfer requirements by Chinese entities (both government and private) did not rank among the top 10 challenges faced by the Council's members in 2010. Among U.S. firms where technology was an issue, when asked if their company had been asked to transfer technology to China over the past three years, 18% answered yes. Among the respondents that had been asked to transfer technology, 20% said the pressure came from a government entity, while 80% said that it came from a Chinese company.[117] Of the respondents who said they were asked to transfer technology, 40% stated that they found the requests acceptable, 30% refused the requests, 15% negotiated to mitigate the amount of technology transfer, and 10% said they had to transfer the technology requested in order to gain access to the Chinese market.[118] As noted by the U.S.-China Business Council, China

> has a long-term strategy to bring in foreign technology. But technology is not simply "given to China." Instead, technology is typically licensed to a China-based entity in which the foreign company has an ownership stake. In many cases the foreign company owns 100 percent of the entity in China; in some cases, the foreign company must form a joint venture with a Chinese partner. In exchange, the company determines a value of the technology to be transferred and negotiates a payment--the technology is rarely "given" for free.[119]

Press reports indicate that the USTR's office is currently seeking information from U.S. manufacturers on examples of efforts by the Chinese government to force the transfer of technology from U.S. companies operating in China. This issue was discussed during President Obama's meeting with Chinese Vice President Xi Jinping on February 14, 2012.[120] A White House Factsheet of the meeting stated: "China reiterates that technology transfer and technological cooperation shall be decided by businesses independently and will not be used by the Chinese government as a pre-condition for market access."

In the 112th Congress, S. 2063 (Webb) would prohibit the transfer by a U.S. commercial entity of any proprietary technology or intellectual property that was researched, developed, or commercialized using a contract, grant, loan, loan guarantee, or other financial assistance provided or awarded by the U.S. government to certain foreign entities (such as those that are owned or controlled by a foreign government) unless the Secretary of Commerce determined (and issued a waiver) that the transfer would not compromise the U.S. economic interests or competitiveness.

Cyber Security Issues

Cyber attacks against U.S. firms have raised concerns over the potential large-scale theft of U.S. IPR and its economic implications for the United States. A 2011 report by McAfee stated that its investigation had identified targeted intrusions into more than 70 global companies and warned that "every conceivable industry with significant size and valuable intellectual property has been

---

[117] However, the Council notes that since the Chinese government maintains approval authority for investment decisions, which may be used by Chinese firms as leverage when attempting to negotiate technology transfer agreements with U.S. firms.

[118] Ibid.

[119] U.S. China Business Council, *USCBC 2011 China Business Environment Survey Results: Market Growth Continues, Companies Expand, But Full Access Elusive for Many,* November 2011, p.20.

[120] Inside Trade, *USTR Seeks Info From Manufacturers On Forced Technology Transfer To China,* January 31, 2012.

compromised (or will be shortly), with the great majority of the victims rarely discovering the intrusion or its impact."[121] Many U.S. analysts and policymakers contend that the Chinese government is a major source of cyber-economic espionage against U.S. firms. For example, Representative Mike Rogers, chairman of the House Permanent Select Committee on Intelligence, stated at an October 4, 2011, hearing that

> attributing this espionage isn't easy, but talk to any private sector cyber analyst, and they will tell you there is little doubt that this is a massive campaign being conducted by the Chinese government. I don't believe that there is a precedent in history for such a massive and sustained intelligence effort by a government to blatantly steal commercial data and intellectual property. China's economic espionage has reached an intolerable level and I believe that the United States and our allies in Europe and Asia have an obligation to confront Beijing and demand that they put a stop to this piracy.[122]

According to a report by the U.S. Office of the Director of National Intelligence (DNI): "Chinese actors are the world's most active and persistent perpetrators of economic espionage. U.S. private sector firms and cyber security specialists have reported an onslaught of computer network intrusions that have originated in China, but the IC (Intelligence Community) cannot confirm who was responsible." The report goes on to warn that

> China will continue to be driven by its longstanding policy of "catching up fast and surpassing" Western powers. The growing interrelationships between Chinese and U.S. companies—such as the employment of Chinese-national technical experts at U.S. facilities and the off-shoring of U.S. production and R&D to facilities in China—will offer Chinese government agencies and businesses increasing opportunities to collect sensitive US economic information.[123]

China's Obligations in the World Trade Organization

Negotiations for China's accession to the General Agreement on Tariffs and Trade (GATT) and its successor organization, the WTO, began in 1986 and took over 15 years to complete. During the WTO negotiations, Chinese officials insisted that China was a developing country and should be allowed to enter under fairly lenient terms. The United States insisted that China could enter the WTO only if it substantially liberalized its trade regime. In the end, a compromise was reached that required China to make immediate and extensive reductions in various trade and investment barriers, while allowing it to maintain some level of protection (or a transitional period of protection) for certain sensitive sectors. China's WTO membership was formally approved at the WTO Ministerial Conference in Doha, Qatar, on November 10, 2001. On November 11, 2001, China notified the WTO that it had formally ratified the WTO agreements, and on December 11, 2001, it formally joined the WTO.[124]

---

[121] The report did not indentify China (or any country) as the source of the intrusions. McAfee, *Revealed: Operation Shady Rat, An Investigation of Targeted Intrusions Into More Than 70 Global Companies, Governments, and Non-Profit Organizations During the Last Five Years*, 2011.

[122] House Permanent Select Committee on Intelligence, *Chairman Mike Rogers Opening Statement at the Hearing on Cyber Threats and Ongoing Efforts to Protect the Nation*, October 4, 2011.

[123] DNI, Office of the National Counterintelligence Executive, *Foreign Spies Stealing U.S. Economic Secrets in Cyberspace, Report to Congress on Foreign Economic Collection and Industrial Espionage*: 2009-2011, October 2011.

[124] Following China's WTO accession, the United States, in January 2002, granted China permanent normal trade relations (PNTR) status (prior to that time, that status was on a conditional basis) to ensure that the United States and (continued...)

Under the WTO accession agreement, China agreed to

- reduce the average tariff for industrial goods from 17% to 8.9%, and average tariffs on U.S. priority agricultural products from 31% to 14%;

- limit subsidies for agricultural production to 8.5% of the value of farm output, eliminate export subsidies on agricultural exports, and notify the WTO of all government subsidies on a regular basis;

- within three years of accession, grant full trade and distribution rights to foreign enterprises (with some exceptions, such as for certain agricultural products, minerals, and fuels);

- provide non-discriminatory treatment to all WTO members, such as treating foreign firms in China no less favorably than Chinese firms for trade purposes;

- end discriminatory trade policies against foreign invested firms in China, such as domestic content rules and technology transfer requirements;

- implement the WTO's Trade-Related Aspects of Intellectual Property Rights (TRIPS) Agreement upon accession (which sets basic standards on IPR protection and rules for enforcement);

- fully open the banking system to foreign financial institutions within five years (by the end of 2006); and

- allow joint ventures in insurance and telecommunication (with various degrees of foreign ownership allowed);

WTO Implementation Issues

Getting China into the WTO under a comprehensive trade liberalization agreement was a major U.S. trade objective during the late 1990s. Many U.S. policymakers at the time maintained that China's WTO membership would encourage the Chinese government to deepen market reforms, promote the rule of law, reduce the government's role in the economy, further integrate China into the world economy, and enable the United States to use the WTO's dispute resolution mechanism to address major trade issues. As a result, it was hoped, China would become a more reliable and stable U.S. trading partner. U.S. trade officials contend that in the first years after it joined the WTO, China made noteworthy progress in adopting economic reforms that facilitated its transition toward a market economy and increased its openness to trade and FDI. However, beginning in 2006, progress toward further market liberalization appeared to slow. By 2008, U.S. government and business officials noted evidence of trends toward a more restrictive trade regime.[125] The USTR's 10th annual report to China on WTO compliance (issued in December 2011) identified several areas of concern, including[126]

- failure by the Chinese government to maintain an effective IPR enforcement regime (discussed below);

(...continued)

China had a formal trade relationship under the rules of the WTO.

[125] China generally implemented its tariff reductions on schedule.

[126] USTR, *2011 Report to Congress on China's WTO Compliance*, December 2011.

- industrial policies and national standards that attempt to promote Chinese firms (while discriminating against foreign firms);

- restrictions on trading and distribution rights;

- discriminatory and unpredictable health and safety rules on imports (especially agricultural products); and

- burdensome regulations and restrictions on services, and failure to provide adequate transparency of trade laws and regulations.

As of May 2012, the United States has brought 12 dispute settlement cases against China, several of which have been resolved or ruled upon.[127] China has brought six WTO cases against the United States as well.[128] The U.S. cases are summarized below.

Pending U.S. Cases Against China

- On March 13, 2012, the United States, Japan, and the European Union jointly initiated a dispute settlement case against China's restrictive export policies (such as quotas, tariffs, and minimum export prices) on rare earths and two other minerals.[129]

- On September 15, 2010, the USTR's office announced it was bringing a WTO case against China over its improper application of antidumping duties and countervailing duties on imports of grain oriented flat-rolled electrical steel from the United States.

- On September 15, 2010, the USTR's office announced it was bringing a WTO case against China over its discrimination against U.S. suppliers of electronic payment services.

Resolved Cases or a WTO Panel Has Issued a Ruling[130]

- On June 23, 2009, the United States brought a case against China's export restrictions (such as export quotas and taxes) on raw materials (bauxite, coke, fluorspar, magnesium, manganese, silicon metal, silicon carbide, yellow phosphorus, and zinc). The United States charges that such policies are intended to lower prices for Chinese firms (steel, aluminum, and chemical sectors) in order to help them obtain an unfair competitive advantage. China claims that these restraints are intended to conserve the environment and exhaustible natural resources. In July 2011, a WTO panel issued a report that China's export taxes and quotas on raw materials violated its WTO commitments. It further found that

---

[127] For an overview of the WTO's dispute settlement process, see CRS Report RS20088, *Dispute Settlement in the World Trade Organization (WTO): An Overview*, by Jeanne J. Grimmett

[128] China has brought five cases against the United States. These have included challenges to U.S. applications of antidumping and countervailing measures, restrictions on imports of Chinese poultry, and U.S. safeguard measures restricting imports of Chinese tires.

[129] For additional information on China's restrictions on rare earths, see CRS Report R42510, *China's Rare Earth Industry and Export Regime: Economic and Trade Implications for the United States*, by Wayne M. Morrison and Rachel Tang.

[130] Often, cases are resolved through consultations before a case goes to a panel.

China failed to show that restrictions were linked to conservation of exhaustible natural resources for some of the raw materials or to protect the health of its citizens (by reducing pollution).[131] China appealed the WTO panel's ruling. However, on January 30, 2012, a WTO Appellate Body affirmed that China's export quotas and export taxes on certain raw materials violated its WTO commitments.[132] U.S. Trade Representative Ron Kirk called the decision a "tremendous victory for the United States," and said that it would ensure that "core manufacturing industries in this country can get the materials they need to produce and compete on a level playing field."[133]

- On December 22, 2010, the USTR's office announced that it would bring a WTO case against China over a government program that extended subsidies to Chinese wind power equipment manufacturers that use parts and components made in China rather than foreign-made parts and components. On June 7, 2011, the USTR's office announced that China had agreed to end these subsidies. However, the USTR noted that it had taken significant investigatory efforts by the U.S. government, working with industry and workers, to uncover China's wind subsidies because of the lack of transparency in China. The USTR further noted that under the terms of China's WTO accession, it was required to report on all of its subsidy programs, which, to date, it has failed to do.[134]

- On December 19, 2008, the USTR filed a WTO case against China over its support for "Famous Chinese" brand programs, charging that such programs utilize various export subsidies (including cash grant rewards, preferential loans, research and development funding to develop new products, and payments to lower the cost of export credit insurance) at the central and local government level to promote the recognition and sale of Chinese brand products overseas. On December 18, 2009, the USTR announced that China had agreed to eliminate these programs.

- On March 3, 2008, the USTR requested WTO dispute resolution consultations with China regarding its discriminatory treatment of U.S. suppliers of financial information services in China. On November 13, 2008, the USTR announced that China had agreed to eliminate discriminatory restrictions on how U.S. and other foreign suppliers of financial information services do business in China.

- On April 10, 2007, the USTR filed a WTO case against China, charging that it failed to comply with the TRIPS agreement (namely in terms of its enforcement of IPR laws). On January 26, 2009, the WTO ruled that many of China's IPR enforcement policies failed to fulfill its WTO obligations. On June 29, 2009, China announced that it would implement the WTO ruling by March 2010.

---

[131] A summary of the WTO panel report can be found at http://www.wto.org/english/tratop_e/dispu_e/cases_e/ds394_e htm#bkmk394r.

[132] The Appellate Body declared moot and of no legal effect the Panel's findings regarding China's export licensing requirements, minimum export price requirements, administration and allocation of export quotas, and fees and formalities in connection with exportation because of inadequacies in the complainants' panel requests involving these measures.

[133] USTR, *Press Release*, January 31, 2012.

[134] USTR *Press Release*, June 7, 2011, available at http://www.ustr.gov/about-us/press-office/press-releases/2011/june/china-ends-wind-power-equipment-subsidies-challenged.

- On April 10, 2007, the USTR filed a WTO case against China charging that it failed to provide sufficient market access to IPR-related products, namely in terms of trading rights and distribution services. In August 2009, a WTO panel ruled that many of China's regulations on trading rights and distribution of films for theatrical release, DVDs, music, and books and journals were inconsistent with China's WTO obligation. China appealed the decision, but lost, and in February 2010 stated that it would implement the WTO's ruling.

- On February 5, 2007, the USTR announced it had requested WTO dispute consultations with China over government regulations that give illegal (WTO-inconsistent) import and export subsidies to various industries in China (such as steel, wood, and paper) that distort trade and discriminate against imports.[135] China's WTO accession agreement required it to immediately eliminate such subsidies. On November 29, 2007, China formally agreed to eliminate the subsidies in question by January 1, 2008.

- On March 30, 2006, the USTR initiated a WTO case against China over its use of discriminatory regulations on imported auto parts, which often applied the high tariff rate on finished autos (25%) to certain auto parts (which generally average 10%). The USTR charged that that the purpose of China's policy was to discourage domestic producers from using imported parts and to encourage foreign firms to move production to China. On February 13, 2008, a WTO panel ruled that China's discriminatory tariff policy was inconsistent with its WTO obligations (stating that the auto tariffs constituted an internal charge rather than ordinary customs duties, which violated WTO rules on national treatment). China appealed the decision, but a WTO Appellate Body largely upheld the WTO panel's decision.

- On March 18, 2004, the USTR announced it had filed a WTO dispute resolution case against China over its discriminatory tax treatment of imported semiconductors. The United States claimed that China applied a 17% value-added tax (VAT) on semiconductor chips that were designed and made outside China, but gave VAT rebates to domestic producers. Following consultations with the Chinese government, the USTR announced on July 8, 2004, that China agreed to end its preferential tax policy by April 2005. However, the USTR has expressed concern over new forms of financial assistance given by the Chinese government to its domestic semiconductor industry.

During his State of the Union Address in January 2012, President Obama announced plans to create a new Trade Enforcement Unit "charged with investigating unfair trade practices in countries like China." On February 28, 2012, President Obama issued an executive order establishing the Interagency Trade Enforcement Center within the USTR's office. Many analysts contend that the new enforcement unit could result in a sharp increase in the number of WTO dispute settlement cases brought by the United States against China.

---

[135] Some programs gave tax preferences, tariff exemptions, discounted loans, or other benefits to firms that met certain export performance requirements, while others gave tax breaks for purchasing Chinese-made equipment and accessories over imports.

China's Accession to the WTO Government Procurement Agreement (GPA)

Government procurement policies are largely exempt from WTO rules, except for those members which have signed the GPA.[136] When China joined the WTO, it indicated its intention to become a member of WTO's GPA as soon as possible, but, to date, has failed to submit an offer acceptable to current GPA members.

China's accession to the GPA is a major U.S. priority. Estimates of the value of annual Chinese public procurement range from $88 billion to $200 billion.[137] However, China has established a number of restrictive government procurement practices and policies that favor domestic Chinese firms. Because of China's rapidly growing economy and significant infrastructure needs, China's accession to the GPA could result in significant new opportunities for U.S. firms

China did not formally enter into negotiations to join the GPA until 2007, and its initial offer was deemed unacceptable by the other WTO GPA parties. China promised to revise its GPA offer, but did not do so until July 2010. That offer was deemed an improvement over the previous offer but was not accepted, in part because it excluded purchases by local and provincial governments as well as SOEs. A revised offer in December 2011 only covered public entities in three cities and two provinces.[138] Commenting on China's latest offer, the USTR's office stated:

> China began its negotiations to join the GPA four years ago this month. Since that time, China has submitted three offers, each an improvement over the last. But China still has some distance to go before the procurement that it is offering is comparable to the extensive procurement that the United States and other Parties cover under the GPA. For example, we are urging China to cover state-owned enterprises, add more sub-central entities and services, reduce its thresholds for the size of covered contracts, and remove other broad exclusions.[139]

Congressional concerns over China's restrictions on public procurement and failure to join the GPA have resulted in the introduction of legislation in 112th Congress. H.R. 375 (Kildee) would limit the total value of Chinese goods that could be procured by the U.S. government to the same value of U.S. goods procured by the Chinese government in the previous year, while H.R. 2271 (Royce) would prohibit the federal government from awarding contracts to Chinese entities until China signs the GPA. China pledged in May 2012 to make a new GPA offer sometime in 2012.

---

[136] The GPA is a plurilateral agreement among 41 WTO members (including the United States, Japan, and the 27 members of the European Union) that effectively provides market access for various non-defense government procurement projects to signatories to the agreement. Each member of the Agreement submits lists of government entities and goods and services (with thresholds and limitations) that are open to bidding by firms of the other GPA members. WTO members that are not signatories to the GPA, including those that are GPA observers (such as China), do not enjoy any rights under the GPA. Nor are non-GPA signatories in the WTO generally obligated to provide access to their government procurement markets.

[137] Testimony of Karen Laney, Acting Director of Operations, U.S. International Trade Commission before the Subcommittee on Terrorism, Nonproliferation, and Trade, Committee on Foreign Affairs, on *China's Indigenous Innovation, Trade, and Investment Policies*, March 9, 2011.

[138] Inside U.S. Trade, December 8, 2011.

[139] USTR Press Release, December 2011.

China's Currency Policy[140]

Unlike most advanced economies (such as the United States), China does not maintain a market-based floating exchange rate. Between 1994 and July 2005, China pegged its currency, the renminbi (RMB) or yuan, to the U.S. dollar at about 8.28 yuan to the dollar.[141] In July 2005, China appreciated the RMB to the dollar by 2.1% and moved to a "managed float," based on a basket of major foreign currencies, including the U.S. dollar. In order to maintain a target rate of exchange with the dollar (and other currencies), the Chinese government has maintained restrictions and controls over capital transactions and has made large-scale purchases of U.S. dollars (and dollar assets).[142] According to the Bank of China, from July 2005 to July 2009, the dollar-yuan exchange rate went from 8.27 to 6.83 yuan per dollar, an appreciation of 21.1%.[143] However, once the effects of the global financial crisis became apparent, the Chinese government halted its appreciation of the RMB and subsequently kept the yuan/dollar exchange rate relatively constant at 6.83 from July 2009 to June 2010 in order to help limit the impact of the sharp decline in global demand for Chinese products.

Many U.S. policymakers, labor groups, and business representatives of import-sensitive industries have charged that, despite minor reforms, the Chinese government continues to actively intervene in currency markets to keep the value of the RMB artificially low against the dollar. They claim that this policy provides an indirect subsidy to Chinese exporters (which makes Chinese goods less expensive in the United States), while acting as a de facto tariff on U.S. goods imported into China (which makes them more expensive). They argue that this policy has particularly hurt several U.S. manufacturing sectors that are forced to compete against low-cost Chinese products and has led to significant job losses in the United States, especially in manufacturing. Critics further charge that China's currency policy has been a major factor in the size and growth of the U.S. trade deficit with China. Some Members of Congress contend that, given the current high rate of unemployment in the United States, Chinese "currency manipulation" can no longer be tolerated.

Chinese officials have insisted that the current currency policy is not meant to favor exports over imports, but instead to foster domestic economic stability.[144] They have expressed concern that abandoning the currency policy, especially given the current state of the global economy, could further weaken its export industries and cause wide-scale layoffs of Chinese workers. Chinese officials view economic stability as critical to sustaining political stability. They further note that China's global trade surplus has declined sharply over the past few years.

On June 19, 2010, the Chinese central bank, the People's Bank of China (PBC) stated that, based on current economic conditions, it had decided to "proceed further with reform of the RMB

---

[140] For additional information on this issue, see CRS Report RS21625, *China's Currency Policy: An Analysis of the Economic Issues*, by Wayne M. Morrison and Marc Labonte.

[141] The official name of China's currency is the renminbi, which is denominated in units of yuan.

[142] Much of China's trade is believed to be in U.S. dollars (e.g., exporters are often paid in dollars). The central government requires firms to exchange most of their dollars for RMB.

[143] Calculated from Bank of China data using the official middle rate.

[144] A fixed (or pegged) exchange rate is a relatively common practice among developing countries, especially those that want to attract foreign investment and expand exports. A constant exchange rate, such as one tied to the U.S. dollar, attempts to signal foreign investors that the value of their investments will not be affected by the type of large swings in exchange rates that can occur under a floating exchange rate regime. Given the current size of China's economy and trade flows, most economists question whether the continuation of China's currency policy is appropriate.

exchange rate regime and to enhance the RMB exchange rate flexibility." Since that time, according to Treasury Secretary Timothy Geithner, the RMB has risen by 13% in real terms against the dollar and by 40% (in real terms) overall since 2005. U.S. officials have urged China to continue to appreciate its currency, but at a more rapid pace.

Numerous bills have been introduced in Congress over the past few years that would seek to induce China to reform its currency policy or would attempt to address the perceived effects that policy has on the U.S. economy. For example, one bill in the 108th Congress would have imposed an additional duty of 27.5% on imported Chinese products unless China appreciated its currency to near market levels. In the 111th Congress, the House passed an amended version of H.R. 2378 (Tim Ryan), which would have made certain misaligned currencies (such as the RMB) actionable under U.S. countervailing duty cases on foreign government export subsidies (although the Senate did not take up the bill). The bill was re-introduced in the 112th Congress in the House and Senate (see H.R. 639 and S. 328, discussed below).

Currency Legislation in the 112th Congress

- S. 1619 (Sherrod Brown) which passed the Senate on October 11, 2011, by a vote of 63 to 35, would provide for the identification of fundamentally misaligned currencies and require action to correct the misalignment for certain "priority" countries. The bill would require the Treasury Department to issue a semiannual report to Congress on international monetary policy and currency exchange rates, determine which major global currencies are in fundamental misalignment, and designate certain misaligned currencies for priority action. Treasury would be required to seek negotiations with countries designated for priority action. If efforts were not made to correct the currency misalignment, the following actions would be taken in regard to that country: (1) The Commerce Department would be required to factor in the estimated level of currency undervaluation when determining antidumping duties; (2) the President would be required to prohibit the procurement by the federal government of products or services from the country unless it is a party to the WTO's GPA; (3) the Overseas Private Investment Corporation (OPIC) would not be able to approve any new financing (including insurance, reinsurance, or guarantee) with respect to a project located within the country;[145] (4) the U.S. Executive Director at each multilateral bank would be told to oppose the approval of any new financing to the government of a country, or for a project located within a country, that issues a currency designated for priority action. If a country that has a currency designated for priority action failed to take steps to eliminate the fundamental misalignment within 360 days after its designation by the Treasury Department, the following would occur: (1) the USTR would be required to initiate a dispute resolution case against the priority country, and (2) the Treasury Department would be required to consult with the Federal Reserve System to consider undertaking remedial intervention in international currency markets. The bill would also amend U.S. countervailing duty law to require the Commerce Department to initiate an investigation to determine whether currency undervaluation is providing, directly

---

[145] This provision would not affect China because OPIC is already prohibited by U.S. law from operating in China.

or indirectly, a countervailing subsidy and makes clarifications to U.S. countervailing law similar to provisions in H.R. 639 and S. 328.

- H.R. 639 (Sander Levin) and S. 328 (Sherrod Brown) would make a "fundamentally undervalued currency" an actionable subsidy under U.S. countervailing duty law (dealing with government export subsidies).[146] The bills would seek to clarify that a fundamentally undervalued currency could be treated by the Department of Commerce as a benefit conferred by a foreign government to its exports.[147] In addition, the bill seeks to clarify that, in the case of a subsidy relating to a fundamentally undervalued currency, the fact that the subsidy (i.e., the undervalued currency) may have also benefitted non-exporting firms (in addition to exporting firms), would not, for that reason alone, mean that the subsidy could not be considered to be a measure that is contingent upon export performance. The bill directs the Commerce Department to use, if possible, data and methodologies utilized by the IMF to estimate the real effective exchange rate undervaluation of the currency for the purposes of assessing countervailing duties.[148] Factors used to determine a fundamentally undervalued currency would include (over an 18-month period): protracted and large-scale intervention in currency markets; a real effective exchange rate estimated to be undervalued by at least 5%; and foreign asset reserves held by the government that are (1) greater than the amount needed to repay its debt obligations over the next year, (2) 20% of the nation's money supply, and (3) the value of the country's imports over the previous four months.

- S. 1130 and S. 1267 (both by Rockefeller) would, among other things, treat "exchange rate manipulation" as an actionable subsidy under U.S. countervailing duty cases. Exchange rate manipulation would be defined as protracted large-scale intervention by a country to undervalue the country's currency in the exchange market that prevents effective balance-of-payments adjustment or that gains an unfair competitive advantage over any other country.

- S. 1238 (Olympia Snowe) would require that, before Congress approves any bill implementing a free trade agreement or extending permanent normal trade relations status to another country, the President would have to first certify that the government of the potential trading partner has not, in the 10 years preceding the certification, manipulated its currency for the purposes of gaining an unfair advantage in international trade.

Some Members has expressed opposition to various currency bills, arguing that they violate U.S. obligations in the WTO. Other Members have argued that while inducing China to adopt a market-based exchange rate is an important goal, the United States should give higher priority to addressing China's industrial policies and IPR infringement, which some view as more damaging to U.S. economic interests.

---

[146] These bills are identical and are the same legislation passed by the House (H.R. 2378) in September 2010. The Senate did not take up the bill.

[147] The benefit would be defined as the difference between the amount of foreign currency received by the exporter from the transaction and the amount that would have been received if the currency was not undervalued.

[148] For a summary of U.S. trade remedy laws, see CRS Report RL32371, *Trade Remedies: A Primer*, by Vivian C. Jones.

The U.S.-China Strategic and Economic Dialogue

On September 29, 2006, President George W. Bush and Chinese President Hu Jintao agreed to establish a Strategic Economic Dialogue (SED) to have discussions on major economic issues at the "highest official level." According to a U.S. Treasury Department press release, the intent of the SED was to "discuss long-term strategic challenges, rather than seeking immediate solutions to the issues of the day," in order to provide a stronger foundation for pursuing concrete results through existing bilateral economic dialogues.[149] The first meeting was held in December 2006. Four subsequent rounds of talks were held (the last was in December 2008).

While attending the G-20 summit in London on the global financial crisis on April 1, 2009, President Obama and Chinese President Hu agreed to continue the high-level forum, renaming it the U.S.-China Strategic and Economic Dialogue (S&ED). The new dialogue is based on two tracks. The first (the "Strategic Track") is headed by the Secretary of State on the U.S. side and focuses on political and strategic issues, while the second track (the "Economic Track") is headed by the U.S. Treasury Secretary on the U.S. side and focuses on financial and economic issues. Areas of discussion include economic and trade issues, counterterrorism, law enforcement, science and technology, education, culture, health, energy, the environment (including climate change), non-proliferation, and human rights.

One of the reported benefits of the S&ED process is that it brings together top economic officials from both sides, as well as U.S. cabinet officials and Chinese heads of ministries, on a regular basis, which enables both sides to identify their major positions and priorities on various issues and to develop long-term working relationships. Some in Congress have criticized the S&ED forum, arguing that it produces few concrete results, and that many of the results described in subsequent fact sheets that are jointly issued simply re-state agreements or pledges China has already made. Others counter that U.S. engagement with China occurs on multiple levels throughout the year and that the S&ED meetings are in part a cumulative result of this process.

The July 2009 Economic Track Session

The first round of the S&ED was held in Washington, DC, on July 27-28, 2009, and involved 12 U.S. Cabinet officials and agency heads and 15 Chinese ministers, vice ministers, and agency heads. The session was focused heavily on issues relating to the global economic crisis. Secretary of the Treasury Timothy Geithner stated: "Recognizing that cooperation between China and the United States will remain vital not only to the well being of our two nations but also the health of the global economy, we agreed to undertake policies to bring about sustainable, balanced global growth once economic recovery is firmly in place."

The two sides agreed to establish a framework of cooperation based on four pillars:

- Advancing macroeconomic and structural policies to achieve sustainable and balanced growth;

- Promoting more resilient, open, and market-oriented financial systems;

- Strengthening trade and investment ties; and

---

[149] U.S. Treasury Department press release, December 15, 2006.

- Strengthening the international financial architecture.

These pillars appear to have been aimed at deepening bilateral cooperation in response to the global economic crisis, continuing commitments on both sides to promote policies that seek to achieve more balanced economic growth, encouraging China to continue economic and financial reforms, expanding China's role and/or participation in international economic forums,[150] and attempting to avoid new forms of trade protection.

May 2010 Economic Track Session

The May 24-25, 2010, S&ED economic session focused heavily on the continuing efforts relating to the four pillars indentified in the July 2009 session. Although few concrete accomplishments were announced at the end of the meetings, the two agreed to intensify talks on a number of bilateral economic and trade issues. The two sides pledged to

- Sign a cooperation protocol on small and medium-sized firms (SMEs);

- Boost economic cooperation at the central and local government level, such as promoting the establishment of state-to-province and city-to-city partnerships;

- Conduct "intensive expert and high-level discussions" as early as the summer of 2010 on innovation issues (such as China's indigenous innovation proposals) and to take into account the results of these talks in formulating and implementing their innovation measures;[151]

- Improve cooperation to address health and safety issues relating to U.S. sales of soybeans to China;

- Establish a cooperative mechanism between the U.S. Export-Import Bank and the Export-Import Bank of China on trade finance, and to develop initiatives to promote exports by SMEs;

- Explore the possibility of cooperating to enable the United States to treat China as a market economy, and to treat certain Chinese firms as market-oriented industries, for the purpose of U.S. trade remedy laws; and

- Boost investment opportunities and transparency.[152]

---

[150] The United States is seeking to broaden China's participation in international economic institutions in order to promote the goal of helping to make China a "responsible stakeholder" in the global economy. This implies that, since China greatly benefits from the global trading system and is a major global economy, it should shoulder a greater responsibility in maintaining and promoting that system (rather than just enjoying the benefits of that system

[151] The United States also pledged that it would review Chinese concerns relating to U.S. restrictions on high technology exports to China resulting from the current U.S. export control regime.

[152] The United States pledged that it welcomed investment from China and confirmed that review of foreign investment by the Committee on Foreign Investment in the United States ensures the consistent and fair treatment of all foreign investment without prejudice to the place of origin. China promised to revise its Catalogue Guiding Foreign Investment in Industries and encourage and expand areas open to foreign investment, including those relating to high-technology, energy, and the environment. China also pledged to streamline the process for investment approval.

The May 2011 Economic Track

The third round of the S&ED was held in Washington, DC, on May 9-10, 2011. Prior to the meeting, U.S. officials identified several goals for the economic track of the S&ED, including ensuring that China followed through on previous economic and trade commitments (such as on IPR protection and indigenous innovation policies) and encouraging China to make a number of reforms to its financial sector (such as adopting market-based interest rates on bank deposits and expanding market access in China for U.S. financial firms). China pledged to continue to promote domestic consumption, improve IPR enforcement, eliminate all of its indigenous innovation products catalogues, improve transparency of its economic and trade policies, and provide significant new opportunities for U.S. financial services firms in China.

The May 2012 Economic Track

The fourth S&ED round was held in Beijing on May 3 and 4, 2012, and focused largely on economic rebalancing and boosting foreign access to China's financial services sector.[153] China pledged that it would:

- Increase the number of SOEs that pay dividends;

- Participate in negotiations (beginning in the summer of 2012) for new rules on official export financing with the United States and other major exporters;

- Provide non-discriminatory treatment to all enterprises, regardless of type of ownership, in terms of credit, taxation, and regulatory policies so that U.S. firms can more easily compete against Chinese SOEs;

- Submit a new robust offer in 2012 to join the WTO's GPA and to intensify efforts to negotiate a BIT with the United States;

- Open up more sectors to FDI and improve the transparency of its investment approval process;

- Prioritize the protection of trade secrets, extend efforts to promote the use of legal software by Chinese enterprises, treat IPR owned or developed in other countries the same as IPR owned or developed in China, and hold discussions with U.S. officials on the implementation of China's commitment not to make technology transfer a pre-condition for doing business in China;

- Take steps to raise household income and lower prices of consumer goods, such as cutting import tariffs, reducing taxes on services, and raising deposit rates;

- Expand market access to domestic financial markets by boosting the permitted level of foreign investment in its stock and bond markets, raising the permitted foreign equity stake in domestic securities joint ventures from 33% to 49%, and allowing foreign investors to establish joint venture brokerages to trade commodity and financial futures (with up to a 49% equity stake).

---

[153] The session was somewhat overshadowed by events relating to Chinese human rights advocate Chen Guangcheng who had been temporarily sheltered at the U.S. embassy in Beijing prior to the session.

Concluding Observations

China's rapid economic growth and emergence as a major economic power have given China's leadership increased confidence in its economic model. The key challenges for the United States are to convince China that (1) it has a stake in maintaining the international trading system, which is largely responsible for its economic rise, and to take a more active leadership role in maintaining that system; and (2) further economic and trade reforms are the surest way for China to expand and modernize its economy. For example, by boosting domestic spending and allowing its currency to appreciate, China would likely import more, which would help speed economic recovery in other countries, promote more stable and balanced economic growth in China, and lessen trade protectionist pressures around the world. Improving IPR protection in China and providing non-discriminatory treatment to foreign IP firms would likely foster greater innovation in China and attract more FDI in high technology than under what has occurred under current policies. Lowering trade barriers on imports would increase competition in China, lower costs for consumers, and boost economic efficiency. Some observers contend that reformist-minded officials in China will continue to push for greater free-market reforms, while others argue that vested interests in China (such as SOEs and export-oriented firms) who benefit from the status-quo will make further economic reforms more difficult to realize.

Opinions differ as to the most effective way of dealing with China on major economic issues:

- Some support a policy of high-level engagement with China using various forums, such as the U.S.-China S&ED, in order to try to resolve complex and long-term issues and prevent either side from imposing new protectionist measures.

- Others support a somewhat mixed policy of using engagement with China when possible, coupled with greater use of WTO dispute settlement procedures to address China's unfair trade policies. Some Members contend that the S&ED forum has failed to produce many tangible results and have advocated using the S&ED to induce China to agree to measurable targets or goals for reducing trade and investment barriers and improving IPR measures that can be used in future meetings to determine China's progress.

- Still others, who see China's economic policies as damaging to U.S. economic interests, advocate a more aggressive U.S. trade policy towards China that uses all available tools available to U.S. policies, including multilateral institutions (such as the WTO and International Monetary Fund), as well as U.S. trade remedy laws (such as antidumping and countervailing measures) to counter the negative effects of China's "unfair trade practices."[154] Some Members have

---

[154] On March 13, 2012, President Obama signed into law H.R. 4105 (P.L. 112-99), which clarifies that U.S. countervailing duty law can be applied to subsidized goods from nonmarket economy countries (such as China), and that the Department of Commerce can adjust antidumping duties applied to goods from nonmarket economy countries when countervailing duties are applied to the same goods. The measure was enacted in response to a December 2011 Court of Appeals decision that held that U.S. law prohibits the Department of Commerce from applying countervailing duties to non-market economies and to comply with a WTO ruling over applying both countervailing and antidumping measures on imports. See CRS Report RL33976, *U.S. Trade Remedy Laws and Nonmarket Economies: A Legal Overview*, by Jeanne J. Grimmett.

---

argued that the United States should insist on trade and investment reciprocity with China to ensure a more "balanced" economic relationship.

Author Contact Information

Wayne M. Morrison
Specialist in Asian Trade and Finance
wmorrison@crs.loc.gov, 7-7767